PAINTINGS & DRAWINGS
AT WILTON HOUSE

PHAIDON

Rembrandt: *Portrait of the artist's mother* (Cat. No. 124)

A CATALOGUE OF
THE PAINTINGS & DRAWINGS
IN THE COLLECTION AT
WILTON HOUSE
SALISBURY · WILTSHIRE
COMPILED BY
SIDNEY, 16TH EARL OF PEMBROKE

PHAIDON · LONDON ~ NEW YORK

© 1968 PHAIDON PRESS LTD · 5 CROMWELL PLACE · LONDON SW7

PHAIDON PUBLISHERS INC · NEW YORK
DISTRIBUTORS IN THE UNITED STATES: FREDERICK A. PRAEGER INC
III FOURTH AVENUE · NEW YORK · N.Y. 10003
LIBRARY OF CONGRESS CATALOG CARD NUMBER: 68-18902

SBN 7148 1323 0

MADE IN GREAT BRITAIN
PRINTED BY HUNT BARNARD AND CO LTD · AYLESBURY · BUCKS

CONTENTS

INTRODUCTION

THE Collection at Wilton is one of the oldest in England. No manuscripts have survived to show exactly when it was begun, or what pictures were bought, but it can be dated from the beginning of the reign of James I, when William, 3rd Earl of Pembroke, and his younger brother Philip, 1st Earl of Montgomery (and later 4th Earl of Pembroke as well), were respectively Lord Steward and Lord Chamberlain to the King.

Up to that time, pictures by foreign painters, apart from portraits, were virtually unknown in England. Tudor houses like Wilton, and those built in the reign of James I, contained family portraits, tapestries, hangings and armour. William Herbert, founder of the family and builder of the house on the site of the Abbey given to him by Henry VIII, whose son Edward VI created him Earl of Pembroke, would have had his portrait painted, as well as one of his wife, Ann Parr, sister of Catherine. Their son Henry, 2nd Earl, and his three wives would also have been painted; the famous Mary Sidney, his third wife and mother of the 3rd and 4th Earls, must have sat for the Court painters, though no portraits of her have survived, with the possible exception of a small painting at Penshurst, where she lived as a child. But there are engravings and prints after lost portraits, one by Cornelius Johnson. The Tudor and early Jacobean portraits which surely must have been at Wilton were almost certainly burnt in the fire of 1647, which destroyed so much of the house.

It is supposed, though there are no records of their travels, that William, 3rd Earl, and his brother Philip, on their visits to the Continent saw paintings by Italian, French, Dutch, Flemish, and German masters, and were duly impressed. It is frustrating not to know whether they bought pictures on their own and had them shipped to England, or whether they employed agents later to buy for them. But there is evidence that by the time James I died in 1625, they already had in their possession some pictures of considerable interest. The invaluable catalogue of the Royal Collections by Abraham van der Doort states: '*Item, a little St George, wch yor Matie had in exchange of my Lord Chamberlaine for the booke of Holbins drawings wherin manie heads were done wth Cryons wch my Lor Chamblaine imediatly soe soone as hee receaved it of yor Matie gave it to my Lor: Marshall in a ebbone & speckled woodeden frame, painted upon the right lighte. Done by Raphaell Urbin.*' St George and the Dragon by Raphael is now in the National Gallery of Art, Washington. The catalogue also gives a full description of a portrait of a '*full faced painted younge woman's picture. . . . wch your*

Matie togeither with the 2 children of Permencius had in a way of exchange for a little Judith of Rafell Urbin when you were Prince, of the late decd Lo: of Penbrooke Steward of your Maties household . . . , done by John Bellin, chaunged by yor Matie when you were Prince.'

Miniatures by Hilliard and others were also exchanged, and it is amusing to imagine the meetings and discussions about works of art in London and at Wilton, which Charles I and Henrietta Maria often visited, between the brothers and their Royal master, and their excitement as packing-cases containing new treasures arrived.

After the death of William, 3rd Earl, in 1630, Philip, now Lord Pembroke, continued to hold the office of Lord Chamberlain, and Van der Doort worked under him. The purchases and exchanges of pictures went on, but by then the competition was fierce within the small circle of rich and powerful nobles at Court, the most famous being Buckingham, Arundel and Hamilton, to acquire the masterpieces from the Continent.

The arrival in England of Rubens and Van Dyck added to the growing appreciation of foreign painters, as well as to the desire of the courtiers to be painted by the 'new' artists. The fact that the King, having first claim on their services, commissioned a very large number of Royal portraits, meant that others had to wait their turn. To cope with the commissions, many talented assistants were no doubt taken on in the studios, working under their master's supervision, and to them fell the task of painting much of the backgrounds as well as the dresses.

Van Dyck's large studio was near Blackfriars, and Lord Pembroke and his family, and probably the King as well, must have paid frequent visits to it, though some of the portraits may have been painted inside the Palace of Whitehall, or in Durham House (off the Strand), where Lord Pembroke lived when he did not stay at Wilton with his numerous children.

The great group of the Herbert family, containing ten life-size figures, measures eleven feet in height, and seventeen feet in length; it was begun in 1634–5, and finished in 1636. Perhaps it was painted in Durham House, where it hung for sixteen or seventeen years before being moved to Wilton (which must have presented quite a problem) after Inigo Jones and John Webb had finished building and decorating the 'Double Cube' room, designed to take it and nine other Van Dyck portraits of the family, the King, the Queen, and their three eldest children.

How were pictures moved from London to the country before the advent of railways and motor-cars? The only way was by wagon or farm cart, the picture rolled up if on canvas, taking weeks on rough, dusty or wet roads; how much damage was caused it is impossible to say. Only pictures four or five feet high and wide could have got inside a private, stage or mail coach.

But to return to the early days of the Pembroke Collection, there is in the British Museum (Egerton MS. 1636) a list of ' *The Earl of Pembrookes Collections of Paintings at Durham House, Mr Towers keepes them*', which included three Titians, a Correggio, a Giorgione, two Andrea del Sartos, a Jacopo Palma, the four seasons by Bassano, a Tintoretto, and other Italian Masters, and '*a mighty large piece of the Ea: of Pembrooke and all his family by Vandyke, and divers Ladyes by Vandyke, many having two Ladyes in a Piece*'.

The list and notes were made by Richard Symonds, who visited various collections on his return from Italy, and the date is 1652–3. A note at the end says, '*others most or all to be sold and divers already sold*'.

As the contents of Durham House were taken to Wilton after the reconstruction by Inigo Jones and John Webb following the fire of 1647, it is possible that, together with the family portraits by Van Dyck, a few of the paintings mentioned were retained, as the collection today includes *Christ washing the Disciples' feet* by Tintoretto, *Soldiers disputing over Christ's garments* by Jacopo Palma, and the *Virgin and Child, St John and two angels* by Andrea del Sarto.

Among the manuscripts at Hatfield, which Lord Salisbury has allowed me to consult, is a folio size book of one hundred and eleven pages of the executors' accounts of Philip, 4th Earl of Pembroke, dated 1650–5, in which is recorded the sale of a considerable number of pictures sold to various people: '*my Lady Devonshire, the Spanish Ambassador, Lord Bellasis, Sir James Palmer, Mr Tenier, a Dutchman* [who paid £535 for pictures]. The prices ranged from £21 to £350, apart from the transaction with Tenier, but the folio does not say what the pictures were, referring always to 'the particulars in the picture book', which unfortunately is no longer at Wilton. On January 22nd, 1649/50, is the following entry: '*Paid to Mr Lilly, painter, one bill signed by Mr Towers* [who was paid £20 a year to look after the pictures at Durham House and Baynards Castle] *for severall pictures made for the late Earl of Pembroke, the sum of eighty five pounds, being by the hands of Mr Anthony Gratiane, and assented unto by the Executors that he might be serviceable in the sale of pictures.*' These paintings by Sir Peter Lely would probably be of William, later 6th Earl of Pembroke, as a child, James Herbert and his wife, and perhaps Catherine, second wife of Philip, 5th Earl.

The Civil War undoubtedly reduced the family income considerably, and the cost of rebuilding, decorating and furnishing Wilton must have been enormous, so that Philip was forced to sell much of the collection formed by his father and his uncle. It was perhaps at this time or soon after that the great group of drawings by Holbein, already referred to, now at Windsor, were sold, only one being retained because the sitter George Nevill, 5th Lord Abergavenny, had been a friend and contemporary Welsh neighbour of the 1st Earl.

Philip, the 5th Earl of Pembroke, did not take a very active part in public life, but he was a member of the Court of Charles II, at whose Coronation in 1661 he bore the Spurs. In 1669 (he died in December of that year) he received an unexpected gift of paintings from Cosimo III, Grand Duke of Tuscany, whom he entertained at Wilton; an account of this visit is given by a Count Magalotti in 'Journal des voyages faits par Come III en 1669' in a manuscript in the Laurentian Library in Florence. The Grand Duke's gift consisted of the following paintings:

The Virgin and Child, St John, and a young woman and child: Andrea del Sarto.
Mary Magdalen: School of Titian.
A Piper: Savoldo.
The Holy Family: Parmegianino.
Offering of the three Kings: School of Paolo Veronese.
A woman with a dog: Correggio.
The Holy Family: Palma Vecchio.
The Ascension: Baldassare Peruzzi.

Gambarini, on page 89 of his catalogue, says that these eight 'were a present to Philip (father of Earl Thomas) from the Duke of Florence, who, when Prince of Tuscany, had been with him at Wilton three or four weeks'.

The first five are still at Wilton; the attributions to Andrea del Sarto and Parmegianino were correct, although the *Piper,* by Savoldo, was given to Giorgione, *Mary Magdalen* to Titian, and the *Offering of the Three Kings* to Veronese. The *Woman with a dog,* if it was by Correggio, was little more than a wreck, and was sold at Christie's on June 22, 1951, lot 16, for £273. The Palma Vecchio and the Peruzzi have disappeared.

The gift was no doubt a very welcome addition to the collection and considered of first class importance. But it would not be unfair to assume that, when visits to foreign countries such as England were to be made, someone like the Grand Duke would have given orders for a number of his less good pictures to be packed up for travelling, or for copies to be made by his Court painters which he could take with him. It is today of great interest to be able to record that five of the paintings in the collection were given by a Medici in the seventeenth century.

John Evelyn visited Wilton in 1654, but apart from recording that he saw some fine pictures and the Hunting panels by Pierce, his observations on the collection are negligible. John Aubrey, who was born in Wiltshire and knew Wilton well, contented himself with writing scandalous gossip about the family, singling out Mary Sidney and her brother, who were dead before he was born; he made no reference to the pictures.

The next information about the contents of Wilton is contained in an inventory made

Sir Anthony van Dyck: *Philip, 4th Earl of Pembroke, and his Family* (Cat. No. 158)

on November 16, 1683, three months after the death of Philip, 7th Earl of Pembroke, who was a dissolute character and a spendthrift; he had married Henriette de Querouaille, sister of Louise, Duchess of Portsmouth, and they had one daughter.

This inventory accounts for no less than two hundred pictures, put down as follows:

12 pictures called ye 12 Cesars	12. 00. 0.
1 picture of Henry 7th, 1 of Henry 8. 1 of Henry 4 of France	20. 00. 0.
1 ,, ,, Wm ye first Earle of Pembrooke, 1 of his Son	
1 of ye Earle of Essex, 1 of Sr Robt Dudley, 1 of James King of Scots	30. 00. 0.
1 of old King Charles on horseback	80. 00. 0.
1 of phaeton in his chariott and of his man	110. 00. 0.
9 pictures	4. 00. 0.
6 ,,	12. 00. 0.
11 ,,	24. 00. 0.
8. ,,	42. 00. 0.
25 more and some mapps	45. 00. 0.

In the picture Gallery.

58. pictures	435. 00. 0.
17. ,,	15. 00. 0.
9. ,,	28. 00. 0.
36. ,,	154. 00. 0.
4. ,,	5. 00. 0.
17. ,,	35. 00. 0.
1 over the chimney	20. 00. 0.
7. Pictures	80. 00. 0.

Having given this scant information on paintings, the inventory proceeds to describe in great detail a mass of tapestries, beds and hangings which are no longer at Wilton. As Lord Pembroke died in debt, they were probably all sold, but it will never be known how many of the paintings were sold, or what they were.

'*Wm ye first Earle of Pembrooke*' is undoubtedly the full-length portrait of him now at Wilton, and possibly '*I of old King Charles on horseback*' is the little oil-sketch by Van Dyck of the Duc D'Epernon, as there is some facial resemblance and similarity in style to the equestrian portrait of Charles I.

Thomas, the brother who succeeded in 1683 as 8th Earl, was a man of very different character; serious-minded, learned, industrious, he was a statesman as well as a patron of the arts, and he set about the task of restoring the family fortunes, and of adding on a very large scale during the next fifty years to the collection at Wilton. His interests were very wide, a huge library was formed, several hundred pieces of antique sculpture were bought, as well as a famous collection of ancient coins and medals, and the number of paintings by foreign artists was largely increased. At the end of his long life, in 1731, two years before he died, a certain Count Carlo Gambarini of Lucca visited Wilton and compiled the first catalogue under the direction of Lord Pembroke. In his introduction he says that there was an old catalogue (which no longer exists) of the pictures *'collected by the first Earl who lived in four reigns, and by the first two Philips. This Lord [Thomas] has not increased the number, he has only changed many Jerman and Flanders to make a greater variety of Italian Painters. Here are except two or three of above twenty remarkable painters, and of Van Dyke many, because the Great room has only of him, only one of each painter; three quarters of them are by Italian, here being with those that are in London, near three hundred Italian painters ending with the chief disciples of each school, none but such as were alive before the death of Carlo Maratti; of these there were above thirty, they may be easily known by their names to have been the disciples of Carlo Maratti, Carlo Dulci, Giardano of Naples, Albani, and of Cervelli of Venice; these were bespoke when Sir And. Fountaine was in Italy. . . .'*

That is all that is known about the pictures when Earl Thomas was buying, and perhaps exchanging with other collectors in England and on the Continent. He has left no records, so it is not known whether he left the arrangements and the choice to Sir Andrew Fountaine alone, or whether others also acted for him. He may have travelled himself for this purpose; he did go abroad on Government business from time to time, and may have combined business with the pleasure of collecting in foreign studios, galleries and private houses as well as sale rooms, if they existed. The famous Wilton Diptych (now in the National Gallery) *'was given out of the Crown'*, so Gambarini records, *'by King James II to the Lord Castlemain when he went Ambassador to Rome, and bought since he dy'd by Thomas, Earl of Pembroke.'*

In the introduction to the Index volume of the George Vertue notebook, it is said that *'as a collector of miscellaneous jottings he reigns supreme; as an historian of the Arts, he might well have failed'*. His notes on the visits he paid to Wilton in 1716, 1731, and 1740, during the lifetime of the 8th and 9th Earls, bear this out, and he was apt to repeat himself, and indeed on occasions contradicted himself. He rarely expressed an opinion of his own on any particular picture. He jotted down the stories about the collection as told to him by his hosts, and one example can be given how the history of a painting can be recorded differently in less than a hundred years, which is that of the *St George* by Raphael, mentioned at the beginning of this introduction. Van der Doort clearly stated that Charles I exchanged it with Philip, 4th Earl of Pembroke, for the book of Holbein drawings, but as told to Vertue by Thomas, 8th Earl of Pembroke, Balthazar Castiglione gave it to Philip, who exchanged it with Charles I for a Van Dyck group of the Royal Family, which was never painted. This was on the occasion of Vertue's first visit in 1716. More than twenty years later, he visited the 9th Earl, and in one of his entries said that Philip, 4th Lord Pembroke *'recommended Lely to Charles Ist, who had the St. George by Raphael from the E. of P. and gave him for it the book of Holben's drawings of heads, and the Lord Pembr: gave it immediately to the Earl Marshall'.*

Vertue noted that there were portraits of the Herbert family in other houses he visited, such as Penshurst, Knole, Windsor Castle, Cornbury, Hatfield, Warwick Priory, Gorhambury, Bulstrode and Longleat, and in most cases the pictures are there today.

Notes by Vertue like these are of great interest, but do not add to the information about the collection at Wilton. If he had asked the 8th and 9th Earls how, when and where the paintings and drawings were collected, and jotted this down, how invaluable it would have been.

There is one really interesting entry (Vol. IV, p. 185), which reads: *'A sketch very slightly done of a Family peece by Van Dyck sold in Mr Jarvis'* [Charles Jervas, the painter] *sale, bought by Ld. P, on a ½ sheet of paper, by me supposed to be the first thoughts for the gt. family peece of the E. of P. much differing from that as is painted; also in the collection of drawings is just such a drawing with the pen at Ld. Egmont's, possibly the original sketch by Van Dyck.'* Underneath is Vertue's rough sketch of this drawing, which may be the small sketch by or after Lely (now in the possession of Mr Cottrell-Dormer at Rousham) for his very different version which is in the Hermitage collection at Leningrad. What Vertue saw is certainly not the sketch by or after Van Dyck at Holkham.

Vertue did a drawing of Thomas, Lord Pembroke (reproduced in Vol. V, p. 101), as an old man wearing a sort of turban and a long robe or dressing-gown, the body rather bent and his arms folded across his chest. On it Vertue has written *'Th. Er. Pembroke, the manner of habit as I saw him'*, and underneath Horace Walpole has added *'This is very exact and like him'*.

Gambarini, the son of a Lucchese painter, seems to have persuaded Thomas Lord Pembroke to allow him to make a catalogue of the paintings at Wilton – which was to be followed by catalogues of collections in other country houses – and this was published in 1731. Vertue, who may have met him, says (Vol. IV, p. 19) 'a printed book 80. of the collection of pictures by Gambarini but most likely the Lord's own direction – where he proposes'. In other words, Gambarini was told by Lord Pembroke what the paintings at Wilton were, and he duly recorded them in what is the first catalogue to have survived from earlier centuries, and which is therefore of great importance.

But the knowledge of and information about paintings in general was strictly limited, and if anything looked faintly like Raphael, Holbein, Dürer, Giorgione, Titian and other famous names and seemed to be of about the right period, it was labelled accordingly. Both Lord Pembroke and Gambarini accepted the attributions which had either been handed down from previous generations or given when the paintings were bought. But numerous pretty obscure artists at that time were surprisingly credited with their paintings which have stood the test of present day examinations, researches, and general knowledge of the various continental schools. The spelling of their names has sometimes been rather confusing. Subsequent catalogues by Richard Cowdry in 1751, James Kennedy in 1758, and a Mr Richardson in 1774 are virtually repetitions of the Gambarini catalogue, with the additions of purchases made after 1731 and the family portraits commissioned between 1731 and 1774.

The 9th Earl, Henry, of whom such an entertaining account is given in Mr James Lees-Milne's book *Earls of Creation*, was chiefly concerned with architecture. But he did not neglect paintings and commissioned Lambert to paint the set of four landscapes of Westcomb House, Blackheath, which he had built as a summer retreat from London; views of Covent Garden and Lincoln's Inn Fields by Scott; and he bought the landscape by Rubens, and the Mieris self-portrait. He also commissioned the busts of himself and his wife, Sir Andrew Fountaine and Martin Folkes by Roubiliac at a cost of ten guineas each.

His son Henry, 10th Earl, patronized Reynolds, by whom there are nine portraits at Wilton; he commissioned from David Morier the series of equestrian portraits, and from Richard Wilson the views of Wilton, as well as buying three small Italian landscapes by him, a Zuccarelli landscape, his own portrait by Batoni, and various portraits of relations and friends.

Three portraits by Beechey were commissioned by him and by his son, George, 11th Earl, to whom General Goldsworthy bequeathed two seascapes by Van der Velde the Younger, a Teniers, a Netscher, a Francken and two Paters (now in the Frick Collection). The additions in the nineteenth century were confined to family portraits by English artists and, with a few exceptions, portraits only have been added in the twentieth century. The most famous painting in the Wilton Collection, the Wilton Diptych, was sold to the National Gallery in 1929 for £90,000; *Judith and Holofernes* by Mantegna was sold in 1917 to the Widener Collection, and is now in Washington. In 1951 and 1960 some ninety very inferior paintings were sold to permit better arrangements in hanging.

There still remains a collection of nearly two hundred and fifty paintings, apart from the ceilings and mural decorations in oil, and the fifty-five gouache paintings of the Spanish *Haute Ecole*, which have survived two world wars and crippling taxation. Like nearly all the houses in the British Isles where there are collections of paintings which can be enjoyed by the public, Wilton can be visited every year from April till October.

An interval of one hundred and thirty-three years was to elapse between the last eight-eenth-century catalogue of 1774, and the one produced by Nevile Wilkinson in 1907. During that time, most of the paintings had either never been cleaned at all, or had been badly cleaned and restored, so that Wilkinson, who was a soldier by profession and later became Ulster King of Arms, and knew little about paintings, suffered under the handicap of examining the canvases and panels obscured by dirt, repaints and old varnish. Having persuaded my grandfather, who was his father-in-law, to allow him to make a catalogue, he proceeded to do so in two years. The result was an immensely bulky production in two volumes, published in 1907, full of inaccuracies, masses of irrelevant details of family history, bad photographs, and hundreds of heraldic devices and embellished letters, all beautifully done as was to be expected of a member of the College of Arms, to whom a catalogue of paintings seems to have taken second place.

It was therefore necessary to make a new catalogue, but not before the whole collection had been cleaned and examined, and fresh information collated in the light of modern research. All this has taken over thirty years, during which time every painting has also been photographed after cleaning, and in some cases X-rayed as well.

Passavant in 1836, Waagen in 1854 and Scharf at the end of the nineteenth century saw the Wilton collection, but as none of them made any discoveries or added any information about the history or attributions, references to them or comments by them have been omitted, except in a few instances. Similarly, entries in the various *Klassiker der Kunst* volumes were made so long ago and without visual examination, that they, too, with few exceptions, have been omitted.

THE EIGHTEENTH-CENTURY CATALOGUES

GAMBARINI, 1731

A description of the Earl of Pembroke's pictures. Now published by C. Gambarini of Lucca. Being an introduction to his design. Westminster. Printed by A. Campbell, in King Street, near St Margaret's Church. 1731.

★

COWDRY, 1751

A description of the Pictures, Statues, Busto's, Basso-Relievos, and other curiosities at the Earl of Pembroke's House at Wilton. By Richard Cowdry. London. Printed for the Author, and sold by J. Robinson, at the Golden Lion, in Ludgate Street; at Mr Leake's, at Bath, and at Mr Gibb's Glover, at Salisbury. MDCCLI.

★

KENNEDY, 1758

A new description of Pictures, Statues, Bustos, and Basso-Relievos and other curiosities at the Earl of Pembroke's house at Wilton. In the antiques of this Collection are contain'd the whole of Cardinal Richelieu's and Cardinal Mazarine's, and the greatest part of the Earl of Arundel's; besides several particular pieces purchas'd at different times. By James Kennedy, Salisbury. Printed by Benjamin Collins, on the New Canal; and sold by R. Baldwin, in Pater-Noster Row, London. MDCCLVIII.

★

RICHARDSON, 1774

Aedes Pembrochianae: or a critical account of the Statues, Bustos, Relievos, Paintings, Medals, and other antiquities and curiosities at Wilton House, formed on the plan of Mr Spence's Polymetis; the ancient poets and artists being made mutually to explain and illustrate each other. To which is prefixed, an extract of the rules to judge of the goodness of a picture, and the science of a connoisseur in painting. By Mr Richardson. With a complete index, by which any particular Statue, Busto, Painting, etc., and the places or rooms where disposed, may be immediately turned to. London. Printed for R. Baldwin, in Pater-Noster Row. MDCCLXXIV.

★

ACKNOWLEDGMENTS

I HAVE received invaluable assistance from Mr Oliver Millar, Deputy Surveyor of The Queen's pictures, who has done much research on my behalf, particularly in connexion with seventeenth- and eighteenth-century portraits, as well as giving me advice on many points, and I express my most grateful thanks to him.

Mr Martin Davies, Mr Michael Levey and Mr Cecil Gould of the National Gallery have most generously given of their time and expert knowledge of many of the paintings of the foreign schools, and Mr David Piper, formerly Director of the National Portrait Gallery and now Director of the Fitzwilliam Museum, Cambridge, and Professor E. K. Waterhouse, Director of the Barber Institute of Fine Arts, Birmingham, have been equally helpful in connexion with the British eighteenth- and nineteenth-century portraits. To all of them, I wish to give my sincere thanks.

Mr William Mostyn-Owen and Mr David Carritt of Christie's have also given me much advice and made many interesting suggestions, particularly regarding some of the more obscure Italian painters, and I am most grateful to them.

Mr Edward Croft-Murray, Keeper of the Department of Prints and Drawings at the British Museum, assisted by his colleagues, Mr Philip Pouncey and Mr John Gere, have undertaken the whole of the cataloguing of the Drawings, and I cannot thank them sufficiently for doing this most expert work.

Perhaps I would never have made a catalogue of the Collection if it had not been for Sir Kenneth Clark and the Earl of Crawford who, many years ago, stirred my interest in paintings, and suggested that, in due course, I should make an attempt to do so; I expect that they have both forgotten, and that, when they see the result, they may regret the advice they gave me. But I have had enormous pleasure in doing this work, which has brought me in touch with so many interesting, helpful and delightful people at home and abroad, who were most willing to answer inquiries and often produced fascinating information.

January 1, 1968   PEMBROKE

CATALOGUE

NOTE

Unless otherwise stated, the medium is oil. The measurements are given in inches. The catalogue is arranged alphabetically according to Schools, beginning with the Austrian School, and ending with the Spanish, and the names of the painters are arranged alphabetically under each School. The pictures are numbered accordingly. The Ceiling paintings are not numbered or grouped in Schools, and will be found at the end, before the drawings, under the names of the rooms in which they are situated.

The Drawings are listed separately and numbered 1–36 in alphabetical order under the artists' names.

Where the entry under *Provenance* states: 'At Wilton before 1730', it means that the painting is mentioned in Gambarini's Catalogue, which was published in 1731; the other eighteenth-century catalogues by Cowdry, Kennedy and Richardson follow almost exactly Gambarini's entries.

AUSTRIAN SCHOOL

Baron Reis d'Eisenberg

I. SELF-PORTRAIT

Canvas, 32 × 39 in.

Three-quarter length, standing against a table, on which are his books on horsemanship dedicated to Francis I of Austria, to whom he was principal riding-master, and to George II. He wears a dark-blue coat, the edges trimmed with gold and gold bands on the sleeves, with a white cravat of lace, and white lace frilly cuff on the left hand, which rests on one of the books; his right gloved hand is raised holding a long whip, above which is his coat of arms. He wears a white wig. The background is mainly blue, with red curtain behind his head.

The dates of his birth and death are unknown.

Cleaned and repaired in 1948.

Provenance: Probably given by the Baron to Henry, 10th Earl of Pembroke, between 1754 and 1760, about the same time as the set of gouache paintings of the *Haute Ecole* (No. 2). Graves and Cronin say that in the Reynolds Ledger is an entry 'for lining a picture of Isenberg, fifteen shillings' in 1760.

2. HAUTE ÉCOLE: THE SPANISH RIDING SCHOOL: a set of fifty-five Horses and Riders
Plates 139–141

Gouache on paper, backed with wood. Each 10½ × 15 in.

A book of the engravings of the Spanish Riding School by B. Picart after D'Eisenberg is dated 1747, Leipzig.

Provenance: Executed by Baron D'Eisenberg for Henry, 10th Earl of Pembroke, about 1755.

Austrian School, XVIII Century

3. A CAVALRY OFFICER RIDING A GREY CHARGER

Canvas, 20 × 16 in.

The officer, on a grey horse with blue saddle-cloth, faces to the left, and wears a scarlet tunic, breeches and boots, a tall brown fur hat with green leaves on the top and a brown fur slung jacket. Background of a burning village, and blue sky.

Cleaned in 1960.

Provenance: Perhaps acquired by Henry, 10th Earl of Pembroke, or it may have been the property of Count Woronzow, passing on his death to his son-in-law, George, 11th Earl.

School of Johann Baptist Lampi
1750–1830

Portrait painter; born in Austria, but worked for many years in Russia. Died in Vienna.

4. EMPRESS MARIE FEODOROVNA OF RUSSIA (1759–1828)

Canvas, 29½ × 23½ in.

Head and shoulders, turned slightly to the right; she wears a white satin and lace dress, with the ribbon of the Order of St Andrew, and the Star of the Order of St Catherine. On her fair curled hair she wears a small diamond crown.

Re-lined and cleaned in 1935.

The Empress, born Princess Dorothea of Württemberg-Montbéliard, was the second wife of Czar Paul I, and the mother of Czar Alexander I and Czar Nicholas I. She was married in 1776; her husband, who went insane, was murdered in 1801.

Provenance: Left by Count Simon Woronzow in 1832 to his only daughter, Catherine, second wife of George, 11th Earl of Pembroke. On the back of the frame is stamped 'C.P.' with a coronet.

References: Wrongly described by Wilkinson as the Empress Elizabeth, No. 231, French School; identified by A. Polotsoff and other Russian art historians when exhibited at the Russian Art Exhibition at 1 Belgrave Square in 1935, Catalogue No. 819.

BRITISH SCHOOL

William Ashford
1746–1824

Born in Birmingham; settled in Dublin, where he became well known as a landscape painter, and was the first President of the Hibernian Academy in 1823.

5. DUBLIN BAY FROM MOUNT MERRION PARK
Canvas, $35\frac{1}{2} \times 50$ in.

In the foreground are groups of small figures with dogs on a path; horses and deer are seen grazing in the park. Beyond the trees, the sea is visible with Howth and Lambay in the distance.

Mount Merrion House, three miles south of Dublin, came into the possession of the Pembroke family in 1816 through inheritance from Richard, 7th Viscount Fitzwilliam, founder of the Museum at Cambridge, to his cousin, George, 11th Earl, whose grandmother Mary Fitzwilliam married the 9th Earl.

Provenance: Bought by Sidney, 16th Earl of Pembroke, at Christie's, on April 17, 1964, for £2,100. Formerly the property of a gentleman. Another landscape of Mount Merrion Park was bought by the Hon. Desmond Guinness.

Sir William Beechey
1753–1839

Born at Burford, Oxfordshire; entered the R.A. Schools 1772. In Norwich, 1782–7; elected A.R.A. 1793, and R.A. 1798, when he was knighted.

6. THE REVEREND DR THOMAS EYRE (? 1734–1812)
Canvas, 30×25 in.

Head and shoulders, turned slightly to the right, wearing clerical dress.

Repaired and cleaned in 1939. In good condition.

Thomas Eyre was educated at St John's College, Oxford, 1754, and was D.C.L. in 1759. He became Rector of Fovant and Chilmark in Wiltshire, and in 1780 Prebendary of Salisbury Cathedral, and from 1796 to 1812 he was Prebendary of Wells. He married Eleanor, daughter of W. Ingram Michell of Bapton, Wilts., who died in 1771. He was Chaplain to the Pembroke family for a number of years.

Provenance: Probably commissioned by Henry, 10th Earl, or George, 11th Earl of Pembroke; wrongly called by Wilkinson Archdeacon William Coxe. In the Wilton House Inventory of 1827 is the following entry: 'Portrait head of the Rev Eyre. D.D. size of life, Sir Wm. Beechey.'
In Beechey's account book, 1790 – ten guineas.

Reproduced: Henry, Elizabeth, and George, The Pembroke Papers, 1939, as a portrait of Coxe.

7. LADY HERBERT (1766–1793)   *Plate 28*
Canvas, 30×25 in.

Half-length, seated, turned slightly towards her left; wearing a white dress with a blue sash and a white scarf, and a white ribbon in her hair, tied with a bow at the back.

Cleaned and repaired in 1939. In very good condition.

Elizabeth Beauclerk, Lady Herbert, was the second daughter of Lady Diana Beauclerk (eldest daughter of the 3rd Duke of Marlborough) and Topham Beauclerk; she married in 1787 her first cousin George, Lord Herbert, afterwards 11th Earl of Pembroke, and had four children – three sons and a daughter. She died a fortnight after the birth of her last son, in 1793.

Provenance: Commissioned by Lord Herbert, and paid for in 1789. In Beechey's account book (W. Roberts, *Sir William Beechey,* 1907, p. 221. 'ten guineas'). A small version was painted at the same time (five guineas), but its present whereabouts is unknown.

Exhibited: Royal Academy, 1792.

Reproduced: The Pembroke Papers, Vol. II, 1950.

8. CAPTAIN AUGUSTUS MONTGOMERY, R.N.
(1762–1797)   *Plate 29*

Canvas, 30×25 in.

Head and shoulders in naval uniform, with a black
stock; the face is turned slightly to the right.

Cleaned in 1939. In very good condition.

Augustus Montgomery, the natural son of Henry,
10th Earl of Pembroke, and Miss Kitty Hunter
(who later became the wife of Field-Marshal
Alured Clarke), was born in 1762. He was at first
given the name of Retnuh (Hunter reversed) and
then Reebkomp (anagram of Pembroke); on
becoming a Captain in the Navy in 1782, Lord
Pembroke gave him the name of Montgomery,
Lady Pembroke having objected to his being
called Herbert.

He married Miss Susan Malpass c. 1790–1, and there
were children, one son, George Augustus Montgomery, entering the Church.

His last command was H.M.S. *Theseus*, on board
which he died on February 6, 1797.

Provenance: Commissioned by Lord Pembroke or
Lord Herbert; paid for in 1789 (Mr Herbert, ten
guineas; Beechey account book, W. Roberts,
1907, p. 221).

Exhibited: Royal Academy, 1792.

*Reproduced: Henry, Elizabeth, and George, The
Pembroke Papers*, 1939.

Sir Oswald Birley
1880–1952

Portrait painter; lived and worked in London.

9. REGINALD, 15TH EARL OF PEMBROKE, M.V.O.
(1880–1960)

Canvas, 62×42 in.

Standing, turned slightly to the left, nearly full-
length, wearing the uniform of the Royal Horse
Guards (The Blues); in his right gloved hand he
holds his plumed helmet, which is resting against
his slightly bent right knee; in his left gloved hand he
holds his sword. Over his shoulders is draped his
blue and red military cloak.

Signed in the bottom left-hand corner: Oswald
Birley, 1930.

Reginald Herbert was the eldest son of the 14th Earl
of Pembroke and Lady Beatrix Lambton. Educated

at Eton and Sandhurst, and then joined his Regiment, remaining with it until 1919, retiring with
the rank of Lieutenant-Colonel. Mayor of Wilton
in 1932–3. Hereditary Visitor of Jesus College,
Oxford. Married in 1904 Lady Beatrice Paget,
daughter of Lord Alexander Paget, and sister of the
6th Marquess of Anglesey, by whom he had three
sons and one daughter.

Provenance: Commissioned by Lord Pembroke at a
cost of one thousand pounds.

10. SIDNEY CHARLES, LORD HERBERT, LATER
16TH EARL OF PEMBROKE (b. 1906)

Canvas, 30×25 in.

Half-length, turned slightly to the left. He wears a
black suit, with a white collar and grey tie.

Signed in the bottom left corner: 'To Sidney from
Oswald Birley, 1936'.

Provenance: A wedding present from the artist.
Painted in three sittings.

11. THE HON. SIR GEORGE SIDNEY HERBERT, BT.
(1886–1942)

Canvas, 28×23 in.

Half-length, head and body turned slightly to the
right. He wears the Windsor Uniform of dark blue
with red collar and cuffs.

Signed in top right hand corner: Oswald Birley.
1939.

George Herbert was the second son of Sidney, 14th
Earl of Pembroke, and Lady Beatrix Lambton;
educated at Eton and Oxford, he joined the Wilt-
shire Regiment in 1914, and commanded the 4th
(T.A.) Battalion after World War I. Chairman of
the Executive, Conservative Party; Alderman,
Wilts County Council; Gentleman Usher to King
George V, 1928–36, and to King Edward VIII; and
Groom-in-Waiting and Gentleman Usher to King
George VI till his death in 1942. Created a Baronet
in 1937.

Provenance: Commissioned by his brother, Reginald,
15th Earl of Pembroke; on their mother's death in
1944 the painting came into the Wilton Collection.

12. THE 'HOLBEIN' PORCH AT WILTON

Canvas, 35½×27½ in.

The painting shows two of the three decorated sides
of the sixteenth-century stone porch, which, until

James Wyatt removed it to its present site in the garden, was originally inside the great quadrangle of the House as the entrance porch.

Signed in the bottom right hand corner: Oswald Birley, 1931.

Provenance: Painted by Sir Oswald during a week-end visit to Wilton, and presented by him to Lord and Lady Pembroke.

Alfred Edward Chalon
1781–1860

Born at Geneva, moved as a child with his parents to London, where he studied at the R.A. It was as a portrait painter in water-colours that he established his name. He was elected an Academician in 1816. Later in life he took to painting in oil, in which he was not successful.

13. ROBERT, 12TH EARL OF PEMBROKE (1791–1862)

Canvas, $36\frac{1}{2} \times 27\frac{1}{2}$ in.

Half-length, full face, seated, wearing a black frock coat, grey waistcoat, and black cravat. Red background.

Robert Lord Pembroke was the eldest surviving son of George, 11th Earl, and his first wife, Elizabeth Beauclerk. Born in London, he succeeded his father in 1827 and lived mainly in Paris, where he died unmarried.

Provenance: Commissioned by the sitter, and painted about 1837, in which year it was exhibited at the Royal Academy.

Edward Clifford
1844–1907

Portrait painter.

14. THE HON. SIDNEY HERBERT, LATER 14TH EARL OF PEMBROKE. (See No. 82)

Pastel on canvas, 25 × 20 in.

Head and shoulders, turned to the right. Wearing a grey-brown tweed jacket and a red tie.

Signed: Edward Clifford. 1875.

Provenance: Commissioned by George, 13th Earl of Pembroke.

15. THE HON. MICHAEL HERBERT, LATER THE HON. SIR MICHAEL HERBERT (1857–1903)

Fourth son of the Hon. Sidney Herbert; married in 1888, Lelia (Belle) Wilson, daughter of Richard Wilson of New York (see No. 184). Ambassador to Washington, 1902–3.

Pastel on canvas, 34 × 23 in.

Seated, full face, wearing a grey suit, with his left arm by his knee.

Inscribed along the top: MDCCCLXXVI. The Hon. Minga Herbert.

Provenance: Commissioned by George, 13th Earl of Pembroke.

Michael Dahl
1656–1743

Born in Stockholm; settled in England in 1688.

16. BARBARA, COUNTESS OF PEMBROKE (?1675–1722)   *Plate* 13

Canvas, 30 × 25 in.

Head and shoulders, in a feigned oval, full face, wearing a brown and blue satin dress, low cut, with a white frill. Long brown hair. Plain brown background.

Cleaned in 1950. In very good condition.

Barbara, daughter of Sir Thomas Slingsby, 2nd Baronet, married Thomas, 8th Earl of Pembroke, as his second wife in 1708. They had one daughter Barbara, who married William North, of Glenham Hall, Suffolk. Lady Pembroke was first married to John, Lord Arundel, and secondly to Sir Richard Mauleverer, Bt.

Provenance: Probably commissioned by Lord Pembroke at the time of their marriage, 1708.

17. JOHN, 2ND DUKE OF MONTAGU, K.G. (?1688–1749)   *Plate* 122

Canvas, $48\frac{1}{2} \times 39$ in.

Three-quarter length, standing sideways, head turned slightly to the left; he is wearing armour, with a red 'skirt'; his left hand holds the hilt of his sword, and with his right hand he holds a baton, resting on a table with a red cloth, on which is also the helmet. The long grey wig falls to his shoulders. The riband of the Order of the Garter is over his armour. Background of a castle, battle scene and clouds.

Cleaned in 1960. Relined in 1965. In very good condition.

Son of the 1st Duke of Montagu of the first creation; he married Mary Churchill, youngest daughter of the 1st Duke of Marlborough. He was a soldier and a courtier.

It appears that this portrait was finished before 1718, when the Duke received the Garter, as the armour clearly shows underneath.

Provenance: First mentioned in the Cowdry catalogue of 1751; it was probably bought by Henry, 9th Earl of Pembroke, who was a contemporary of the Duke of Montagu.

Versions: At Boughton House (Duke of Buccleuch). At Palace House, Beaulieu (Lord Montagu of Beaulieu).

School of Michael Dahl

18. ALEXANDER POPE (1688–1744)

Canvas, 29 × 24¼ in.

Half-length, seated at a table, head turned to his left, wearing a black dress open at the neck. Short grey wig. In his right hand he holds a quill pen, and his left hand rests on a table on which is a paper and a bottle of ink.

Cleaned in 1951. In fair condition.

Alexander Pope, the poet and satirist, friend of Swift, Addison, and Gay, visited Wilton in 1722. He refers to the 8th Earl's wife in his *Epistles to several persons* (ii) 'To a Lady', and to the Earl himself in (iv) 'To Burlington'. As he lived in a villa at Twickenham, he probably also knew Henry, 9th Earl, who designed, with Roger Morris, Marble Hill for Lady Suffolk.

Provenance: Probably bought by the 8th or the 9th Earl, before 1740.

Versions: At Reading University. The National Portrait Gallery has two oil paintings of Pope, one attributed to Jervas (112) and the other to Richardson (561).

Engravings: In mezzotint by J. Simon (1728) and in line by R. Cooper (1809).

Sir Francis Grant, P.R.A.
1810–1878

Portrait painter; born in Perthshire, worked in London. He was made an A.R.A. in 1842, R.A. in 1851, and President of the Academy in 1866, when he was knighted.

19. SIDNEY, LORD HERBERT OF LEA (1810–1861)
Plate 31

Canvas, 56 × 43½ in.

Three-quarter length, standing, his head turned slightly to his right, wearing a black frock coat, and waistcoat and fawn trousers, with a blue and white spotted cravat round his neck. He has dark hair and a slight beard. In his right hand he holds a paper down by his side, and his left arm rests on a red Government dispatch-box, which is on a table. Background of the wall of a room with books and a curtain.

Cleaned and repaired in 1939. In very good condition.

Sidney Herbert was the only son of George, 11th Earl of Pembroke, by his second marriage to Catherine Woronzow. He entered Parliament in 1833 as Member for South Wiltshire, a post he held until he was made Lord Herbert of Lea two months before his death. He was Secretary to the Admiralty in 1841, Secretary at War in 1845 in Sir Robert Peel's Government, and held the same post under Lord Aberdeen from 1852–5, and under Lord Palmerston from 1859–61. It was through his support of and close association with Florence Nightingale that she was able to establish the nursing service with the Army in the Crimean War.

Provenance: Commissioned by Lady Herbert of Lea after her husband's death in 1861; Grant's correspondence with Lady Herbert at Wilton is undated, but 1862–3 is a probable date for the work; in one letter he sketches out the position, which is identical with the painting, but quite different from the portrait done from life which was presented to the National Portrait Gallery in 1912 by his son, Sidney, 14th Earl of Pembroke (No. 1639). A replica of this is at Wilton. Grant borrowed photographs of him standing, and used drawings in his own book for the earlier portrait. Given or left by Lady Herbert to her grandson, Sir Sidney Herbert, Bt., on whose death in 1939 it came to Wilton.

20. CATHERINE, COUNTESS OF PEMBROKE (1783–1856)   *Plate* 30

Canvas, 50×46 in.

Seated, rather more than half-length, sideways, the head facing to the left; wearing a black dress with white lace collar and cuffs, with a lace cap on her head. A large gold and jewelled brooch holds the lace collar in position; on her left wrist is a gold bracelet, and a gold chain is worn over the dress. Her hands are together on her lap, the left holding a paper, the right a pen. Behind on a table are an inkstand, paper and paper stand. Background of sky on the left and red curtain on the right.

Relined and cleaned in 1950. In good condition.

Countess Catherine Woronzow, the only daughter of Count Simon Woronzow and his wife Katherina Seniavine, was born when her father was the Russian Ambassador in London. Brought up in this country, she married in 1808 George, 11th Earl of Pembroke, as his second wife and was the mother of Sidney, Lord Herbert of Lea, and five daughters, the Marchioness of Ailesbury, the Countesses of Dunmore, Shelburne, Clanwilliam, and Viscountess De Vesci.

Provenance: Painted in 1842; commissioned by Lady Pembroke or her son, the Hon. Sidney Herbert. In Grant's manuscript book of his sitters in the National Portrait Gallery are two entries between July and October: 'The Countess of Pembroke, half length, £157. 10s.'
In September 1844, he made a small copy for one of her daughters, the Countess of Dunmore, for £63.

John Greenhill
1649–1676

Born in Salisbury, and died in London. He was one of Lely's best pupils.

21. THOMAS, 8TH EARL OF PEMBROKE, K.G. (1656–1733)

Canvas, oval, 30×24 in.

Head and shoulders in armour, facing slightly to the left. His long brown wig falls down over his shoulders.

Relined and cleaned in 1939. In good condition.

For biographical details, see No. 134 (Wissing).

Provenance: Painted about 1676, when, as the

Hon. Thomas Herbert, he would have been twenty and the locally born artist twenty-seven, the age at which he died.

Erroneously called 'Henry, Lord Herbert, by Wissing' (Wilkinson, 280); identified by Mr Oliver Millar as by Greenhill.

Version: Northwick Park Collection (E. G. Spencer-Churchill), sold at Christie's, June 25, 1965 (lot 60), for sixty guineas. Previously called James, Duke of Monmouth; correctly identified by Mr Oliver Millar as the 8th Earl of Pembroke by or after Greenhill.

Prince Hoare
1755–1834

Portrait painter, born at Bath, son of William Hoare, R.A., under whom he studied; he then studied at the Royal Academy Schools, and finally in Rome under Raphael Mengs. He was not successful and turned to writing.

22. LADY CHARLOTTE HERBERT (1773–1784)   *Plate* 27

Canvas, oval, 22½×17¾ in.

Half-length, her head turned to the left, wearing a large straw hat, and a low-cut white dress. Over her left arm she carries a basket.

Cleaned in 1951. In very good condition.

Lady Charlotte, the only daughter of Henry, 10th Earl of Pembroke, and Elizabeth Spencer, died of consumption at Aix-en-Provence aged eleven years.
On the back of the canvas is written 'Painted in June 1783'.

Provenance: Commissioned by Lord Pembroke.

William Hoare
1706–1792

Born at Eye, Suffolk; studied for eight or nine years in Italy, and on his return settled in Bath, where he worked mainly in pastel and crayons. One of the foundation members of the Royal Academy.

23. MARY FITZWILLIAM, COUNTESS OF PEMBROKE, AND CUPID

Pastel, oval, 32×27 in.

Seated, in a white dress with a blue 'scarf' and pink ribbons on the sleeves, her hair bound with pearls. Her left arm is across her lap, holding the right arm of Cupid, who has a bow and arrow and leans against her knees. Cupid may be a portrait of her son.

Signed, below the Cupid's wings: Wm. Hoare. Pt.

Mary Fitzwilliam was the eldest daughter of Richard, 5th Viscount Fitzwilliam, of Merrion, Dublin. She married in 1733, Henry, 9th Earl of Pembroke, and had one son, Henry, the 10th Earl. After her husband's death in 1749–50, she married in 1751 Major North Ludlow Bernard, and died in 1769.

Her brother, the 6th Viscount Fitzwilliam, married Catherine, the eldest daughter of Sir Mathew Decker, Bt., in 1744.

Provenance: Commissioned by Henry, 9th Earl of Pembroke, about 1738–40.

The following six pastels are all the same size, 23½ × 17½ in., and were probably done in the same year, 1748, for Henry, 9th Earl of Pembroke.

24. MARY FITZWILLIAM, COUNTESS OF PEM-BROKE

Nearly full face, with a white veil over her head of fair hair; she wears a brown dress with a white lace collar.

25. MRS WRETTLE AS REMBRANDT'S MOTHER

Dressed as in the Rembrandt portrait of his mother. On it is written 'E. Wrettle, Gouvernante to the Hon: Mary Fitzwilliam, Countess of Pembroke. 1748.'

26. SIR ANDREW FOUNTAINE (1676–1753)

Nearly full face, turned to the right, thin white hair; he wears a blue coat with a fur collar.

Of Narford, Norfolk; antiquarian, dilettante, traveller, collector, author, and friend of Swift. He spent much of his time at Wilton, where a room was known as Sir Andrew Fountaine's room, collecting and advising the 8th Lord Pembroke on pictures, books and coins. He continued to act as librarian and custodian of the works of art to the 8th Earl's son Henry, 9th Earl. His bust by Roubiliac, done in 1743, is at Wilton.

27. A YOUNG WOMAN

Her head looks down to the left; she has fair hair with a narrow wreath. Her right arm, behind her head, holds a white drapery, which is also held by her left hand in front of her bare bust.

Probably an imaginary classical figure, which Wilkinson suggests is 'Summer', one of a set of four.

28. A YOUNG WOMAN

In profile, turned to the right; her head is covered with a white turban or cap, held in place by a yellow band. She wears a silvery yellow robe drawn round her, with only her right hand showing.

'Winter', one of a set, as above.

29. THE REVEREND BENJAMIN WOODROFFE. Died 1770.

Nearly full face, wearing a fur cap or hat, and a blue and black coat with a white neck band.

In the Cowdry catalogue of 1751, p. 40, is the entry: 'Here are four pictures in crayons (by Mr Hoare of Bath); the first is of the Reverend Mr Woodroffe of Winchester. . . .'

Mr Woodroffe was a Prebendary of Winchester from 1726 until his death in 1770. He appears also to have been a Chaplain to Lord Pembroke.

When the back of the picture was examined, a small piece of rolled up newspaper fell out of the board fixed to the frame, dated 1748, which confirms that these pastels were all done in that year.

Frank Howard
1805–1866

Son of Henry Howard, R.A. Studied at the Royal Academy, and became an assistant to Sir Thomas Lawrence. He first exhibited at the Academy in 1825, about the time this portrait was painted. In 1842 he moved to Liverpool, where he taught art and lectured, and where he died.

30. PRINCE MICHAEL WORONZOW (1782–1856)
Plate 137

Canvas, 55 × 43 in.

Three-quarter length, standing, his head turned slightly to his right, in the dark blue uniform of a Russian General, with a grey-blue cloak over his right shoulder; his hands are crossed in front, his right hand holding a sword under his left arm. Background of clouds.

Cleaned in 1951. In very good condition.

Michael Woronzow was the son of Count Simon Woronzow, Ambassador in London, and brother of Catherine, Countess of Pembroke. He commanded Russian cavalry against Napoleon. He was Governor-General of the Caucasus, most of which he conquered, from 1823 till shortly before his death, and became a Field-Marshal.

Provenance: The original, by Lawrence, was exhibited at the R.A. in London in 1822, then taken to Russia to the Woronzow house, Alupka, in the Crimea, and now hangs in the Hermitage Gallery, Leningrad. This copy by Howard was painted for Lady Pembroke, and left to her son, Sidney Herbert (Lord Herbert of Lea) on her death in 1856. (Wilton MSS; Catherine Lady Pembroke's list of her possessions.)

Edward Hughes
1833–1908

Born in London, son of the portrait painter George Hughes; exhibited at the Royal Academy; painted a State portrait of Queen Alexandra after the 1902 Coronation.

31. BEATRIX, COUNTESS OF PEMBROKE (1860–1944) AND HER YOUNGEST SON, HON. GEORGE SIDNEY HERBERT (1886–1942)

Canvas, 96×64 in.

Standing, full length, full face; she wears a white dress with a lilac sash, and a long pale-yellow silk coat. A triple pearl necklace round her throat. George Herbert stands beside her, wearing a brown knickerbocker suit, blue tie, pink carnation buttonhole, black buckle shoes, and holds a red bound book with both hands in front. Background of landscape and part of the Palladian Bridge balustrade.
Signed: Bottom left corner, 'Edward Hughes. 1899'.

Lady Beatrix Louisa Lambton was the eldest daughter and one of thirteen children of George, 2nd Earl of Durham, and Lady Beatrix Hamilton, second daughter of the 2nd Duke of Abercorn. She

married in 1877 the Hon. Sidney Herbert, who succeeded his elder brother in 1895 as 14th Earl of Pembroke.
The Hon. George Herbert was created a Baronet in 1937. Died unmarried. (See No. 11.)
Provenance: Commissioned by Sidney, 14th Earl of Pembroke.

Charles Jervas
c. 1675–1739

Born in Ireland, he became a pupil of Kneller, and was a good portrait painter, numbering among his sitters Queen Caroline, wife of George II, Pope, Swift and others. He died in London.

32. HENRY, LORD HERBERT, AFTERWARDS 9TH EARL OF PEMBROKE (1693–1750)

Canvas, 21¼×15 in.

Head and shoulders, turned slightly to the right, long brown hair, wearing a plum-coloured coat with cerise collar and facings; white frill shirt open at the neck; right hand tucked into his coat.

Cleaned in 1961. In very good condition.

For details of 9th Earl see under No. 73.

Provenance: Commissioned by his father, Thomas, 8th Earl, and from his appearance probably painted about 1714, when he was 21.

32A. SIR ANTHONY VAN DYCK

Canvas, 49½×38 in.

Seated to the left, in a high-backed chair covered in a brown material with a purple cloak lying on it, his head turned slightly sideways, he wears a green dress with white and green slashed sleeves, and white collar and lace cuffs, green breeches and stockings. His left arm rests on the arm of the chair, and his right hand holds up a paper. Plain brown background.

Cleaned in 1950. In good condition.

Provenance: Probably bought by Henry, 10th Earl of Pembroke. First recorded in the Richardson catalogue of 1774, p. 49, as in the Chapel, 'the picture of Vandyck by himself'. Wilkinson includes it under School of Van Dyck. The correct attribution to Jervas was made by Mr Oliver Millar in 1964.

Sir Godfrey Kneller
1646–1723

Born in Lubeck; first studied under Ferdinand Bol in Amsterdam, and in 1672 went to Rome, where he was a pupil of Carlo Maratti and Bernini. In 1674 he visited England, where he became a popular portrait painter, and where he decided to settle. He was created a Baronet in 1715.

33. BARBARA, COUNTESS OF PEMBROKE, AND HER DAUGHTER BARBARA

Canvas, 50 × 40 in.

Seated, full face, with her hair down to her shoulders, wearing a low-cut blue-green dress with white edging and ends to the sleeves; her left arm rests on the base of a column, and her right arm is out-stretched with the hand on the head of a lamb, which has a garland round its neck. The child wears a straw hat and a white dress with a red sash, her right shoulder and breast exposed; she holds part of her mother's dress with her right hand, and her left hand is under her mother's right arm. Background of dark sky.

Cleaned in 1960. In fair condition.

For details of Barbara, Lady Pembroke, and her daughter, see No. 16.

Provenance: Commissioned by Thomas, 8th Earl of Pembroke, and painted about 1713.
Mentioned in the Gambarini catalogue, p. 13, which gives no attribution, but states that Lady Barbara is five years old, dressed as a shepherdess.
If this painting is by Kneller, it was done when he was nearly seventy, and parts of it could be the work of his assistants.

George Lambert
1710–1765

Landscape painter; born in Kent. He was a friend of Hogarth and Scott.

34. VIEW OF WESTCOMBE HOUSE, BLACKHEATH
Plate 20

Canvas, 35 × 49 in.

A small square stone house overlooking Greenwich, in a garden or small park, with groups of figures, some with dogs, standing or walking, with the Thames and Greenwich in the distance.

Re-lined, cleaned and repaired in 1932. In good condition.

The figures in this and the other three views are by William Hogarth and the little ships and boats on the Thames are by Samuel Scott. (See J. N. Nichols, *Anecdotes of Hogarth*, 1833, p. 366: 'The Earl of Pembroke has four pictures of Pembroke (sic) House, Blackheath, painted by Lambert, with figures by Hogarth, and shipping by Scott.') Nichols' anecdotes were written from Hogarth's MS.; Hogarth painted Lambert's portrait, and they were great friends.

Westcombe House was built about 1730 by Henry, 9th Earl of Pembroke, perhaps from his own designs, and later in the eighteenth century was leased. It was demolished in 1855.

Provenance: Probably commissioned by Lord Pembroke.

Exhibited: Art Gallery, Birmingham (Richard Wilson and his Circle), Nov. 1948–Jan. 1949, and the Tate Gallery, London, Jan. 1949.

35. VIEW OF WESTCOMBE HOUSE, BLACKHEATH

Canvas, 37 × 48 in.

Looking up at the house from the grounds below.
Re-lined, cleaned, and repaired in 1932. In good condition.

Provenance: As No. 34.

36. VIEW OF WESTCOMBE HOUSE, BLACKHEATH
Plate 21

Canvas, 34 × 48 in.

Looking from the lawn in front of the house towards Greenwich and the Thames, with London in the distance.

Cleaned in 1932. In good condition.

Provenance: As No. 34.

Exhibited: As No. 34.

37. VIEW OF WESTCOMBE HOUSE, BLACKHEATH

Canvas, 37 × 49 in.

Another view of part of the house looking towards Greenwich.

Re-lined, cleaned, and repaired in 1932. In good condition.

Provenance: As No. 34.

Philip de László
1869–1937

38. SIR SIDNEY HERBERT, BT. (1890–1939)

Canvas, $31\frac{1}{2} \times 22$ in.

Half length, side view, the head turned to the left; wearing the khaki uniform of a Lieutenant in the Royal Wiltshire Yeomanry.

Signed in bottom left corner: P. A. de Laszlo. 1915.

The eldest son of the Hon. Sir Michael Herbert, G.C.M.G. (younger brother of the 14th Earl of Pembroke) and Miss Belle Wilson of New York. Educated at Eton and Oxford. Member of Parliament for Scarborough and Whitby 1922–31, and for the Abbey Division of Westminster, 1932–8. He held a number of appointments as Parliamentary Private Secretary. Created a Baronet in 1936. He died unmarried.

Provenance: Commissioned by his mother, and on his death came to the Wilton Collection.

39. MICHAEL GEORGE HERBERT (1893–1932)

Canvas, $31\frac{1}{2} \times 22$ in.

Half length, full face, wearing the khaki uniform of a Second Lieutenant in the Royal Horse Guards (The Blues).

Signed in the bottom left corner: P. A. de Laszlo. 1915.

The younger brother of the above; educated at Eton and Oxford. After the First World War he entered the banking business and became a partner in Morgan, Grenfell & Co. He died unmarried.

Provenance: Commissioned by his mother, and on her death passed to his brother, on whose death it came to the Wilton Collection.

Sir Thomas Lawrence
1769–1830

Born in Bristol; moved to London in 1787, where he met and was influenced by Sir Joshua Reynolds. He soon became a fashionable painter, and George IV, as Prince Regent, patronized him and knighted him in 1815. He became President of the Royal Academy in 1820.

40. COUNT SIMON WORONZOW (1744–1832)
Plate 138

Canvas, 29×24 in.

Head and shoulders, his head turned slightly to the right, wearing a black coat with a white cravat round his neck. Part of a blue riband shows under his coat, and the Star of an Order is on his left breast.

Cleaned in 1935. In very good condition.

Simon Woronzow came from one of the oldest and noblest families in Russia, of Boyar descent. He was appointed by Catherine the Great as her Ambassador in London in 1785. After her death in 1796, he refused to serve the mad Czar Paul I or to return to Russia, but in 1801, when Alexander I succeeded, he was re-appointed. He retired in 1806, but continued to live in London, paying periodic visits to Russia, until his death in 1832. He had married Katherina Seniavine and they had one son, Michael (see No. 30) and one daughter, Catherine (see No. 20), who married, as his second wife in 1808, George, 11th Earl of Pembroke.

Provenance: Commissioned by Count Woronzow, and painted between 1800 and 1806. Lawrence's list of his sitters, at Coutts' Bank, shows that Woronzow owed him £220 between those years. Bequeathed to his daughter, Lady Pembroke. (Wilton MSS.)

Versions: Sir Michael Duff, Bt., Vaynol, North Wales; Hermitage Gallery, Leningrad.

Literature: Sir W. Armstrong, *Lawrence*, 1913, p. 172.

Exhibited: Royal Academy: *The first 100 years.* 1951–2.

Sir Peter Lely
1618–1680

Born at Soest, Westphalia; studied under Frans de Grebber at Haarlem. He came to England in 1641, and had been influenced by Van Dyck, after whose death in that year he became the principal portrait painter. He was knighted in 1680 just before his death.

41. HENRIETTE DE KEROUAILLE, COUNTESS OF PEMBROKE (?1650–1728)
Plate 10

Canvas, 50×40 in.

Full length, seated on a bank, wearing a very low-cut brown satin dress; her right arm is extended holding a flower, while her left hand holds what may be a palm branch. Background of trees in a landscape.

Cleaned in 1932. In very good condition.

Henriette de Kerouaille was the second daughter of Guillaume de Penancoet, Comte de Kerouaille, and married in 1675 Philip, 7th Earl of Pembroke, by whom she had one daughter, Charlotte, who married first John, Lord Jeffreys, son of the Lord Chancellor, and second Thomas, Viscount Windsor. After Lord Pembroke's death in 1683, his widow married in 1685 Thimoléon Gouffier, Marquis de Thois, and died in Paris.

Provenance: Probably painted on her marriage for Lord Pembroke. This portrait was formerly (Wilkinson) called Louise, Duchess of Portsmouth, whom she closely resembled, but it is much more likely that there should be a portrait of Henriette Lady Pembroke at Wilton than of her more notorious elder sister.

Versions: Identical, at Weston Hall, Towcester (Sacheverell Sitwell, Esq.), called the Duchess of Portsmouth. At Althorp, Northants (Earl Spencer), very similar, but the dress is more red-brown in colour, with a blue cloak or shawl falling over the left side, and she sits nearer to the ground: called the Duchess of Portsmouth. Other portraits of her are at Goodwood House (Duke of Richmond) and at La Verrerie in France.

42. THE HON. JAMES HERBERT (1623–1679) AND HIS WIFE JANE SPILLER (about 1625–95)   *Plate 5*

Canvas, 52 × 60 in.

Three-quarter length, standing; he wears a black dress with a white collar, and over his left arm, resting on a pedestal, is a grey cloak; his head is half turned to the left. She wears a low-cut brown dress with a jewelled clasp; over her right arm is a blue cloak, which she holds with her left hand. She is nearly full face with a pearl necklace round her throat. Background of a column, curtain and sky.

Cleaned and repaired in 1950. In good condition.

James Herbert was the sixth surviving son of Philip, 4th Earl of Pembroke, and his wife Susan Vere, daughter of the Earl of Oxford. He married in 1646 Jane, daughter of Sir Robert Spiller of Laleham, Middlesex, and heiress of Tythrop, Oxfordshire. They had four sons and two daughters. James was

Member of Parliament for Malmesbury, and Wiltshire, 1646–8, and Queenborough, 1659–76. He was buried in Thame Church.

Provenance: Presumably painted at about the time of their marriage, 1646–7, and commissioned by Philip, 4th Earl of Pembroke.

43. WILLIAM, 6TH EARL OF PEMBROKE (1640–1674)   *Plate 9*

Canvas, 46 × 50 in.

Full length, naked, sitting at the foot of a tree, his right hand on the head of a brown and white spaniel dog, which sits besides him; a brown cloak is underneath him and partly hides his left thigh and left arm. Background of sky and trees.

Cleaned in 1935. In very good condition.

William, the only child of Philip, 5th Earl, and Penelope Naunton, succeeded his father in 1669, and died unmarried.

Provenance: Commissioned by his father, the 5th Earl, or his grandfather, the 4th Earl; as the boy appears to be aged between four and five years, the painting can be dated about 1645.

44. CATHERINE VILLIERS, COUNTESS OF PEMBROKE AND (?)ONE OF HER DAUGHTERS   *Plate 8*

Canvas, 52 × 60 in.

Lady Pembroke is seated, half turned to the right, wearing a very low-cut grey satin dress, with her hands folded in front, and a pearl necklace and ear-rings. Her daughter stands half turned to the left, wearing a low-cut blue dress; she holds a rope of pearls in her right hand looped over her left wrist, and a pearl necklace and ear-rings.

Catherine Villiers was the daughter of Sir William Villiers of Brookesby, Leicester, and married, as his second wife in 1649, Philip, 5th Earl of Pembroke, by whom she had two sons and five daughters. She died in 1677/8.

Cleaned and repaired in 1950. In good condition.

When this double portrait was cleaned, it was found that it was originally two single portraits, 50 × 40 in., cut down slightly in width. The two were joined together between 1731, when Gambarini mentions it as a single portrait of Lady Pembroke by Lely, and 1751, when Cowdry mentions it as a double portrait of Lady Pembroke and her sister, who is clearly a girl or young woman. The girl is badly drawn and painted, in the style of Lely.

Provenance: Probably commissioned by Lord Pembroke about 1667.

45. CATHERINE, COUNTESS OF ROCKINGHAM (1657–1695)

Canvas, 50 × 40 in.

Three-quarter length, seated on a bank, wearing a low-cut brown dress with white sleeves, and a blue cloak over her shoulders. She is full-face, with light brown curly hair, and has a long ringlet falling down the left side of her neck. In her right hand she holds some small flowers.

Cleaned and repaired in 1951. In good condition.

Catherine Sondes, daughter of the 1st Earl of Feversham (of the first creation), married the Earl of Rockingham in 1677. She was a niece of Catherine Villiers, second wife of Philip, 5th Earl of Pembroke, which would be the reason for this portrait being at Wilton. It was probably painted in the year of her marriage.

It was formerly (Wilkinson) called Eleanor Lady Rockingham, which it could not possibly be in view of the style of dress and date, which is between 1670 and 1680.

Provenance: Perhaps painted for Catherine Lady Pembroke or bought by her.

Versions: At Rockingham Castle (Sir Michael Culme-Seymour) by Lely; at King's Weston; at Burton Hall, Lincoln (Lord Monson).

School of Lely

46. PORTRAIT OF A MAN   Plate 123

Canvas, 50 × 40 in.

Three-quarter length, full face, with a long brown wig; he wears a long brown satin dress, with full white sleeves and a white cravat. His left arm is bent across his chest, and his right arm is bent outwards with the hand on the hip. Background of a column, sky, and landscape with a castle.

Cleaned in 1960. In very good condition.

The sitter was a contemporary of Thomas, 8th Earl of Pembroke, and to have been included in the Wilton Collection, he must have been a close friend, but it has not been possible to identify him.

Mr David Piper has pointed out that the painting can be dated about 1685–90, and the sitter's left hand, right arm, shirt and cloak are borrowed straight from a Lely design, in fact virtually identical with a portrait by Lely of William Wyndham, in the possession of Mr Wyndham Ketton-Cremer. Mr Piper is of the opinion that the Wilton portrait could be by one of Lely's former assistants, or perhaps by Wissing.

Provenance: Bought or commissioned by Thomas, 8th Earl of Pembroke.

David Morier
1705–1770

Painter of portraits, horses, dogs and battle scenes; born in Berne, he came to England in 1743, and died in London.

47. HENRY, 10TH EARL OF PEMBROKE (1734–1794)   Plate 17

Canvas, 48 × 60 in.

On horseback, facing to the right, wearing a scarlet uniform, and a three-cornered hat; to the right is the groom Domenico Angelo, in the Pembroke livery of dark blue with red collar and cuffs, white waistcoat and breeches, holding a horse, with two coupled white dogs at his feet. The figures are represented in an out-door *manège* or riding-school, with a distant view of Wilton and the park and garden in the background.

Cleaned and repaired in 1936. In good condition.

Provenance: Commissioned by Lord Pembroke about 1764–5.

Exhibited: British Country Life throughout the centuries, London, 1937, No. 168.

Reproduced: Henry, Elizabeth and George, The Pembroke Papers, 1939.

48. HENRY, 10TH EARL OF PEMBROKE, AND HIS SON, GEORGE LORD HERBERT

Canvas, 48 × 60 in.

Lord Pembroke is seen wearing a scarlet tunic, and breeches and boots, standing in an open-air riding school. He is facing to the right in front of a horse, which is held by a negro groom wearing the Pembroke livery of dark-blue coat with red collar and cuffs; at his feet is a dog. To the right is his son, wearing a green coat, white breeches and a three-cornered hat, riding a very large horse, facing his father; between them in the background, putting a horse through the paces of the Spanish *Haute Ecole*, is a groom. Behind is a view of the house and park at Wilton. Two more dogs are shown in the left and centre foreground.

Cleaned and repaired in 1936. In good condition.

Provenance: Commissioned by Lord Pembroke about 1764–5.

Reproduced: Henry, Elizabeth and George, The Pembroke Papers, 1939.

49. LIEUT. JOHN (LATER GENERAL SIR JOHN) FLOYD, BT., AN OFFICER OF THE 15TH LIGHT DRAGOONS, AND MISS ELIZABETH HUNTER

Canvas, 48×60 in.

Floyd, of the 15th Light Dragoons, wearing his regimental uniform, is in the centre foreground riding a bay horse facing to the right; to the left in the rear, holding a horse with a side saddle, is Miss Kitty Hunter, Lord Pembroke's mistress; to the right, facing, on a black horse, is another officer of the 15th Light Dragoons. They are seen in an open-air riding *manège* in the park at Wilton; other men and horses are seen in the background.

Cleaned and repaired in 1936. In good condition.

Provenance: Commissioned by the 10th Earl of Pembroke about 1764–5.

Reproduced: Henry, Elizabeth and George, The Pembroke Papers, 1939.

50. HENRY, 10TH EARL OF PEMBROKE, WITH HIS REGIMENT, THE ROYAL DRAGOON GUARDS

Canvas, 49×39 in.

Wearing the scarlet uniform of a General, white and gold waistcoat, white breeches, black jackboots, and a black and gold three-cornered hat, mounted on a white charger, facing to the left. In the background, the Royal Dragoon Guards in review order.

Lord Pembroke was Colonel of The Royals from 1764 till his death in 1794. See also No. 63.

Provenance: From the collection of Lieutenant-Colonel Cortland-Angelo; Michael Angelo, Esq.; Frost and Reed Ltd., from whom it was purchased with the companion picture of Domenico Angelo for £850 in 1959 by Sidney, 16th Earl of Pembroke.

Version: At Windsor Castle, in General's scarlet uniform, riding a white horse, facing to the left.

51. DOMENICO ANGIOLO MALEVOLTI TREMAMONDO (1717–1802)

Canvas, 49×39 in.

Known as Domenico Angelo, born in Italy, settled in England, where he was engaged as a riding-master by Henry, 10th Earl of Pembroke, for the 15th Light Horse, and Royal Dragoon Guards, and for the riding-school at Wilton. In 1755 he married Elizabeth, daughter of Captain Masters, R.N., and in 1761 he opened a fencing school at Carlisle House in London, which became very fashionable.

He is shown here wearing a dark-blue uniform with red collar, and a three-cornered hat, white breeches and jackboots, on a brown horse, facing right, towards a chestnut horse being led by a groom in front of some buildings and trees.

Provenance: See No. 50.

The following ten paintings were either commissioned or bought by Henry, 10th Earl of Pembroke.

52. LIEUT.-GENERAL SIR JAMES CAMPBELL, K.B. (?1670–1745)

Canvas, 19½×16 in.

On horseback, wearing the scarlet uniform of a General, facing to the left, holding a baton in his right hand. Behind him to the right are cavalry, and a battle scene, possibly Dettingen, is in the left background.

Painted in 1744.

Cleaned and repaired in 1939.

Campbell was the third son of the 2nd Earl of Loudon; he was Colonel of the Scots Greys, 1717; Member of Parliament for Ayr, 1727–34; a Groom of the Bedchamber to George II; Governor of Edinburgh Castle, 1738; and Knight of the Bath after the Battle of Dettingen. He died of wounds at the Battle of Fontenoy, where he commanded the cavalry, on April 30, 1745.

Reproduced: Journal of the Society of Army Historical Research, 1939.

53. A GROUP SHOWING VARIOUS BRITISH REGIMENTS (about 1760–4)

Canvas, 19½×23½ in.

L. to R.: Seaman; Foot Guard Drummer; Infantry soldier with green facings (possibly 11th Foot);

Trooper, dismounted, 6th Inniskilling Dragoons; Private, Coldstream Guards; Trooper, 15th Light Dragoons; Artilleryman.

Cleaned and repaired in 1939.

Reproduced: As No. 52.

54. TROOPER, 15TH LIGHT DRAGOONS

Canvas, $19\frac{1}{2} \times 15\frac{1}{2}$ in.

In scarlet uniform, riding a horse galloping to the right, firing a gun.

Painted about 1764.

Cleaned and repaired in 1939.

55. DRUMMER AND TROOPER, 15TH LIGHT DRAGOONS

Canvas, $19\frac{3}{4} \times 15\frac{3}{4}$ in.

Mounted, the drummer facing to the left, the trooper facing the spectator, both wearing scarlet and gold uniforms.

Painted about 1764.

Cleaned and repaired in 1939.

56. TROOPER, 15TH LIGHT DRAGOONS

Canvas, $19\frac{1}{2} \times 15\frac{1}{2}$ in.

On a galloping horse, to the left, firing a musket.

Painted about 1764.

Cleaned and repaired in 1939.

57. TROOPER, 15TH LIGHT DRAGOONS

Canvas, $19\frac{3}{4} \times 15\frac{3}{4}$ in.

On a galloping horse to the right, firing a pistol over his head.

Painted about 1764.

Cleaned and repaired in 1939.

58. TROOPER, 15TH LIGHT DRAGOONS

Canvas, $19\frac{3}{4} \times 15\frac{3}{4}$ in.

Mounted on a prancing white horse, facing to the right, waving a sword over his head.

Painted about 1764, but intended to be 1768; pentimenti on uniform, the green facings having been painted over blue, and white edging to the facings added.

Cleaned and repaired in 1939.

59. MOUNTED MUSICIAN AND TWO DISMOUNTED TROOPERS, 15TH LIGHT DRAGOONS

Canvas, $19\frac{3}{4} \times 15\frac{3}{4}$ in.

The musician faces the spectator, flanked by dismounted troopers, one of which holds a horse on the left.

Painted about 1764.

Cleaned and repaired in 1939.

60. OFFICER'S CHARGER, 15TH LIGHT DRAGOONS, FACING TO THE RIGHT, HELD BY A GROOM IN LIVERY

Canvas, $19\frac{3}{4} \times 15\frac{3}{4}$ in.

Painted about 1764.

Cleaned and repaired in 1939.

61. OFFICER'S CHARGER, 15TH LIGHT DRAGOONS, FACING TO THE LEFT, WITH A GROOM STANDING BEHIND

Canvas, $19\frac{3}{4} \times 15\frac{3}{4}$ in.

Painted about 1764.

Cleaned and repaired in 1939.

William Owen
1769–1825

Born in Ludlow; exhibited in London in 1792, and became a fashionable portrait painter. He was elected a Royal Academician in 1806, and appointed portrait painter to the Prince of Wales in 1810.

62. GEORGE, 11TH EARL OF PEMBROKE, K.G. (1759–1827)

Canvas, 30×25 in.

Head and shoulders, turned slightly to the right, wearing a black coat and white cravat. The Star of the Order of the Garter is on the left breast.

Cleaned and re-lined in 1947. In very good condition.

The only son of the 10th Earl and Lady Elizabeth Spencer, he was educated at Harrow, and after spending five years on the Grand Tour of Europe between 1775 and 1780 with the Rev. William Coxe and Captain John Floyd, he entered the army in the 15th Light Dragoons. In 1784 he became Member of Parliament for Wilton. He commanded his regiment in the Flanders campaign in 1793, succeeded his father in 1794, promoted to Major-General in 1795, Lieutenant-General in 1802, created a Knight of the Garter in 1805, and General in 1812.

He had married in 1787 his first cousin Elizabeth, second daughter of Topham Beauclerk and Lady Diana Spencer, sister of Lady Pembroke. They had three sons, two of whom died as infants, and one daughter, Diana, who married in 1816 the 2nd Earl of Normanton. The eldest surviving son, Robert (see No. 13), succeeded his father in 1827, but died unmarried in 1861. Elizabeth died in 1793, and Lord Pembroke married as his second wife in 1808, Catherine, only daughter of Count Simon Woronzow, Russian Ambassador in London, and by her had Sidney Herbert, later Lord Herbert of Lea, who died in 1861, and five daughters: Elizabeth, who married the 3rd Earl of Clanwilliam; Mary, who married the 2nd Marquis of Ailesbury; Catherine, who married the 6th Earl of Dunmore; Georgina, who married the Earl of Shelburne, later 4th Marquis of Lansdowne; and Emma, who married the 3rd Viscount De Vesci.

Provenance: Commissioned by Lord Pembroke in 1821, and exhibited at the Royal Academy that year.

Versions: A copy, probably by a local artist, is in the Guildhall, Salisbury. Another copy is at Abbey Leix, Ireland (Lord De Vesci).

Sir Joshua Reynolds
1723–1792

Portrait painter; born at Plympton near Plymouth. Apprenticed to Thomas Hudson in 1740 for three years. He was in Italy from 1749–52, then settled in London. First President of the Royal Academy in 1768.

63. HENRY, IOTH EARL OF PEMBROKE, AND HIS SON GEORGE, LORD HERBERT   *Plate* 18

Canvas, 70½×94 in.

Full length, seated in a high-backed chair, his right arm resting on a table, the hand holding a quill pen, and crossed over the left hand, underneath which are some papers; nearby are some books, and another pen in a holder. He is dressed in a scarlet tunic with blue collar and cuffs and white lace frills, white cravat and waistcoat, buff breeches, green stockings,

and black buckle shoes. His son stands, head turned to the right, by his left knee, wearing a dark-blue coat, white waistcoat and breeches, grey stockings, and black buckle shoes. His right hand is in his pocket, and his left rests on the head of a very large dog, round whose neck is a collar on which there is the name 'Earl of Pembroke. 1766'. On the ground beside the dog, in the right corner of the painting, are a saddle, harness and whip. The background behind Lord Pembroke shows the wall of a room with a curtain on the left, and through an open window behind the boy and the dog can be seen a wooded landscape.

Cleaned, re-lined in 1933, and surface cleaning in 1951. In good condition.

For details of Lord Pembroke see No. 65, and of George, Lord Herbert, No. 62.

Provenance: Commissioned by Lord Pembroke, and painted in 1762–3. The receipted bill at Wilton is dated April 16, 1763, and reads as follows: 'The Rt. Hon. The Earl of Pembroke to J. Reynolds Dr. for two whole lengths of Lord and Lady Pembroke. £126. For two heads not yet sent home £42.' (This entry would refer to the portrait of Lord Bristol, No. 67 and the portrait of Charles, Duke of Marlborough, No. 68.) 'Paid for April 15th 1763 Captain Hervey, given to Lord Pembroke £21, and for the Duke of Marlborough £21'. (Reynolds' Ledger.) There are two other entries on the Wilton bill 'for a drawing of the late Lord £2.2.0.; for a sketch of King Charles £5.5.0. and for lining a picture 15/–'. And two payments of eleven and seven guineas to Mr Finey and Mr Meyers.

Reynolds's Sitter books record Lord Pembroke's sittings in March 1757 (four sittings), the year after he was married, when he was twenty-three (and this painting is not one of the Wilton portraits in which he looks older); January 1762; June 1765; January 1767; January 1768 (a note by Reynolds 'March 21st, Lord and Lady Pembroke to be finished'); and June 1783 ('Lord Pembroke paid for miniature 6 guineas'), which is at Wilton.

The son sat in April 1765, June 1766 and May 1767.

The painting of Lord Pembroke, like that of his wife, was of him alone, and when it was decided to add the boy and the dog, Reynolds had to make considerable alterations to the right portion, and pentimenti can clearly be seen in that area, and on the wall behind, where a square picture has been painted out.

Professor E. K. Waterhouse was the first to point out that the boy had been added, and Mr Oliver Millar's close examination confirmed the alterations by Reynolds; the name and date on the dog's collar, 'Earl of Pembroke. 1766' are clearly visible, but this and the alterations were not noticed by Wilkinson, perhaps because they were obscured by dirt and the thick bituminous varnish which Reynolds was so fond of using.

Exhibited: Grosvenor Gallery, 1883–4.

Reproduced: Henry, Elizabeth and George, The Pembroke Papers, 1939.

64. ELIZABETH, COUNTESS OF PEMBROKE (1737–1831)   *Plate* 19

Canvas, 70½×94½ in.

Full length, seated, turned towards the left, wearing a white dress with a pink sash, and over the dress a pink cloak. Her right arm rests on her lap, and her left on a table, over which falls part of a curtain. A pug-dog lies at her feet. Behind her is another table, on which is a work basket. To the extreme left is a large stone urn with a coronet on the top, standing in front of the wall, on which hang two pictures.

Cleaned, re-lined in 1933. In good condition.

Pentimenti on the back wall where square pictures have been substituted for oval ones.

Elizabeth Spencer was the wife of the 10th Earl. For details see No. 66.

Provenance: Commissioned by her husband; for details of sittings see No. 63. Paid for in April 1763. Four sittings.

Exhibited: Grosvenor Gallery, 1883–4.

Reproduced: Henry, Elizabeth and George, The Pembroke Papers, 1939.

Versions: At Blenheim, half-length, turned to the left, wearing a white dress, blue sash, and pink cloak. A similar half length, formerly in the possession of the Earl of Courtown.

65. HENRY, 10TH EARL OF PEMBROKE (1734–1794)   *Plate* 24

Canvas, 50×40 in.

Three-quarter length, facing, wearing scarlet uniform of The Royals, white and blue cravat, buff waistcoat and breeches, his right hand on his sword,

his left arm down by his side. Battle scene in background with clouds.

Cleaned, blisters secured, repaired in 1935 and 1960. In very good condition.

Henry, 10th Earl, was the only child of the 9th Earl and Mary Fitzwilliam. He married in 1756 Elizabeth, daughter of Charles, 3rd Duke of Marlborough, and they had one son, George, and one daughter, Charlotte. Lord Pembroke was a soldier, and a famous horseman, writing books on military equitation. He was Colonel of The Royals from 1764 till his death in 1794. He was also Lord-Lieutenant of Wiltshire.

Provenance: Commissioned by Lord Pembroke; the sittings for this picture took place in 1767–8, together with that of Lady Pembroke and their son (see No. 66) but the bills and receipts are missing.

Exhibited: British Institution 1861; International 1862; Guelph 1891; Reynolds (London) 1937, No. 84, and Plate 28.

Reproduced: Henry, Elizabeth and George, The Pembroke Papers, 1939.

Portraits: Head only, by or after Reynolds, at Somerley, Lord Normanton.
Miniature at Wilton; sat June 1783 'Lord Pembroke paid for miniature 6 guineas.'
Fitzwilliam Museum, Cambridge, as a young man by George Knapton.

Engraving: T. Dixon.

66. ELIZABETH, COUNTESS OF PEMBROKE (1737–1831), AND HER SON GEORGE, LORD HERBERT (1759–1827)   *Plate* 25

Canvas, 50×40 in.

Three-quarter length, seated, turned to her right, wearing a pink dress, with a veil over her head tied under her chin; her son, wearing a brown suit with a white collar, stands by her, his left hand holding hers, and his right a book. A column and red curtain in the background.

Cleaned, blisters secured and repaired in 1934. In very good condition.

Lady Elizabeth Spencer, eldest daughter of Charles, 3rd Duke of Marlborough, and Elizabeth, daughter of Lord Trevor, married in 1756 Henry, 10th Earl of Pembroke. She was a Lady-in-Waiting to Queen Charlotte and one of her closest friends for nearly forty years. She was 94 when she died.

Provenance: Commissioned by Lord Pembroke, 1764–5. Reynolds's Sitter books record the following sittings: Lady Pembroke, January 1764, and Lord Pembroke, June 1765, and the son April 1765, June 1766 and May 1767. These two last dates could be for the large picture with his father (see No. 63). Reynolds painted a second version for Lady Pembroke, without a veil (No. 66A below), which she took to her house, Pembroke Lodge, Richmond Park (which George III built for her). The entry for the sitting may be that recorded in May 1772, and Reynolds's receipted bill at Wilton is for £76, dated May 29th 1773.

Exhibited: British Institution, 1861. International Exhibition, 1862. Guelph Exhibition, 1891. Reynolds (London), 1937, No. 85 and Plate 29. National Loan Exhibition, 1913–14, No. CIV.

Reproduced: Henry, Elizabeth and George, The Pembroke Papers, 1939.

Version: At Wilton, without the veil (see 66A), No. 184 in Wilkinson, and wrongly said by him to be the original or bought by George, 11th Earl; he failed to look at the back of the canvas, on which is written: 'Given by the Countess Dowager of Pembroke to the Wilton Collection of Paintings in June 1828'.

Engraving: J. Watson. (For the purpose of the engraving, this portrait was joined to the one of the husband by himself.)

66A. ELIZABETH, COUNTESS OF PEMBROKE AND HER SON, GEORGE, LORD HERBERT

Canvas, 50×40 in.

Identical to No. 66, but without the veil over her head. The colours have faded considerably.

Cleaned and repaired in 1935. In very good condition.

Provenance: Commissioned by Lord Pembroke or Lady Pembroke in 1772. See No. 66.

Engraving: J. Dixon.

67. AUGUSTUS HERVEY, 3RD EARL OF BRISTOL (1724–1779)   *Plate 133*

Canvas, 30×20 in.

Half-length, in a feigned oval. Full face, wearing naval uniform, with white and gold facings, and a white cravat.

Cleaned in 1939. In very good condition.

Captain Augustus Hervey was a son of John Lord Hervey of Ickworth, Suffolk, and grandson of John, 1st Earl of Bristol. He succeeded his brother in 1775. He was a Captain in the Royal Navy in 1747, becoming Admiral of the Blue, White and Red, and a Lord of the Admiralty in 1775.

Provenance: 'Paid for April 5th 1763' (Reynolds Ledger): 'Captain Hervey given to Lord Pembroke £21.' The receipt for this bill is at Wilton. This is an original repetition from the half-length of 1772 in the Guildhall, Bury St Edmunds.

68. CHARLES, 3RD DUKE OF MARLBOROUGH, K.G. (1706–1758)   *Plate 134*

Canvas, 30×26 in.

Half-length, his head turned to the right, wearing a scarlet uniform with gold facings, black cravat, breastplate, and the Star and Riband of the Garter; a cocked hat is under his arm.

Cleaned in 1950. Relined in 1965. In very good condition.

Charles, 3rd Duke, was a grandson of John, 1st Duke; he married in 1732 Elizabeth, daughter of Thomas, Lord Trevor. Their eldest daughter Elizabeth married Henry, 10th Earl of Pembroke.

Provenance: The Duke gave Reynolds six sittings in 1757, the year after he became Lord Pembroke's father-in-law, and the year before he died. Lord Pembroke commissioned this painting, together with that of Lord Bristol, and the receipt for the two, preserved at Wilton, is dated April 15, 1763, for £42, each painting costing £21.

Engraved: In mezzotint by Richard Houston, as 'J. Reynolds pinx. 1758', and then already in Lord Pembroke's possession.

69. GEORGE, 4TH DUKE OF MARLBOROUGH (1739–1817)   *Plate 135*

Canvas, 50×40 in.

Three-quarter length, standing, with his left arm resting on a pedestal; wearing a white satin dress, white cravat, and a red cloak draped over his right shoulder; a column and sky in the background.

Cleaned in 1950. In good condition.

George, 4th Duke, was the eldest son of Charles, 3rd Duke, and Elizabeth, daughter of Thomas, Lord Trevor. He married in 1762 Lady Caroline Russell, daughter of the 4th Duke of Bedford.

Provenance: Perhaps commissioned by the Duke of Marlborough or his sister, Lady Pembroke, and painted about 1764.

On the reverse of the canvas is written: 'George, Duke of Marlborough by Sir Joshua Reynolds, given to the Wilton collection of paintings by Elizabeth, Countess Dowager of Pembroke and Montgomery in June 1828.'

Versions: At Blenheim (1) 1762, wearing a greeny-blue dress with a red cloak over his left shoulder; (2) at Somerley, Earl of Normanton, three-quarter length, a replica of the Blenheim picture.

70. LORD CHARLES SPENCER (1740–1820)
Plate 136

Canvas, 50 × 40 in.

Three-quarter length, standing, with his left arm resting on the branch of a tree; his right hand holds a hat. He wears a brown coat, waistcoat and breeches, with a white cravat and white ruffles at his wrists.

Cleaned in 1937 and 1964. In very good condition.

Lord Charles was the second son of the 3rd Duke of Marlborough, and younger brother of Elizabeth, Countess of Pembroke. He married in 1762 Mary, daughter of Vere, Lord Vere.

Provenance: Probably commissioned by the Duke of Marlborough, and painted in 1762, the year in which he married. Professor E. K. Waterhouse thinks that it may have originally been given to Lord Bolingbroke but returned to the Duke when Lord Bolingbroke's marriage to Lady Diana Spencer was dissolved in 1768. Or it may have been given to Lady Pembroke, for on the reverse of the canvas is written in black paint 'Lord Charles Spencer, given by the Countess Dowager of Pembroke to the Wilton Collection of Paintings in June 1828'.

Erroneously called Lord Bolingbroke by Wilkinson, who failed to look at the back of the canvas.

Version: At Blenheim, full length, painted in 1759.

By or after Sir Joshua Reynolds

71. HENRY, 10TH EARL OF PEMBROKE

Canvas, 50 × 40 in.

Identical with the portrait of the 10th Earl (see No. 63) and his son, but the curtain on the left is missing. If this is by Reynolds and not a contemporary copy,

it may be the one for which he sat in 1767 and 1768. If it is a copy, it is odd that Lord Pembroke should have had one made as well as the two he commissioned from Reynolds, one of him on his own and the other of him with his son. He may have wanted it to hang in Pembroke House, Whitehall.

72. A DOG

Canvas, 39½ × 50 in.

A black rough-haired retriever stands sideways with his head turned slightly to the right, his left fore-paw off the ground, below which is a dead partridge. To the left is the base of a column, and to the right a waterfall with faint trees behind, and the sky.

Cleaned in 1966.

Provenance: In the 1774 catalogue by Richardson, p. 88, is the entry: 'A favourite dog, by Reynolds', which is the only reason for an attribution to Reynolds. As the catalogue was made in the lifetime of Reynolds and the 10th Lord Pembroke, who was one of his patrons, it is difficult to refute it, but it is not one of Reynolds's best efforts as a painter of animals. It was presumably commissioned by the 10th Earl, about 1770.

Jonathan Richardson
1665–1745

Portrait painter; a pupil of John Riley; rivalled Kneller and Dahl. Author of several well-known books on art.

73. HENRY, LORD HERBERT, AFTERWARDS 9TH EARL OF PEMBROKE (1693–1750)
Plate 15

Canvas, 50 × 40 in.

Three-quarter length, standing, full face, wearing a long red coat, open from the neck to the waist, showing a white frill shirt, a white cravat or scarf round his neck, white cuffs to the sleeves, his left arm resting on a blue cloak over a table, and the right arm on his hip. Background of sky and rocks.

Cleaned and repaired in 1948. In very good condition.

Henry, eldest son of the 8th Earl and Margaret Sawyer, succeeded in 1733, the year in which he married Mary, daughter of the 5th Viscount Fitz-william of Merrion, Co. Dublin. He was known as the Architect Earl, designing with Roger Morris the 'Palladian' Bridge over the river Nadder at Wilton; Marble Hill, Twickenham, for Lady Suffolk, with Morris; a house at Wimbledon for Sarah, Duchess of Marlborough; a water house at Houghton for Sir Robert Walpole; and other buildings; and he superintended the building of old Westminster bridge over the Thames. Mr James Lees-Milne gives a full account of his life in *Earls of Creation* (1962).

Provenance: Commissioned by his father, the 8th Earl, and painted when he was aged about 16, about 1709–10.

74. LADY CATHERINE HERBERT AND THE HON. ROBERT HERBERT   *Plate* 14

Canvas, 50×40 in.

On the left, Lady Catherine is seated on a rock, wearing a blue dress with white sleeves; to the right her brother, Robert, wearing a red dress with sandals, holds a white pigeon in both hands. Background of rocks and sky.

Cleaned in 1950. In very good condition.

Lady Catherine, the eldest daughter of Thomas, 8th Earl, and Margaret Sawyer, was born about 1695, married Sir Nicholas Morice, and died in 1716.

Robert was the second son of his parents, and was born about 1697; he lived at Highclere, Hants, and died in 1763.

Provenance: Commissioned by Thomas, 8th Earl; as they appear to be aged about twelve and ten, the picture was painted about 1709–10 at the same time as the portrait of their elder brother.

Sir William Blake Richmond

1843–1921

Born in London, son of the painter George Richmond; studied at the Royal Academy schools. Exhibited at the R.A. from 1860; elected Academician in 1895.

75. GEORGE ROBERT CHARLES, 13TH EARL OF PEMBROKE (1850–1895)

Canvas, 30×20 in. (Cut down from 56×41 in. in 1965.)

Seated, three-quarter length, turned slightly to the right, the head resting on his upturned right arm, which is supported by a table, on which is a book, his left hand down by his side. He wears a black suit, over which is a fur-lined overcoat. Background of a red curtain.

The eldest son of the Hon. Sidney Herbert and Elizabeth A'Court, he succeeded his uncle in 1862, and married in 1874 Lady Gertrude Talbot, daughter of the 18th Earl of Shrewsbury, but he had no children and died of tuberculosis at the age of forty-five.

Provenance: Commissioned either by Lord Pembroke or his brother; if the latter, it is a posthumous portrait. In a letter at Wilton from the artist, dated 1900, to Sidney, Lord Pembroke, Richmond says he is glad to have had the opportunity of correcting many faults, and that he tried to have it removed from the Academy exhibition, but failed. Presumably Gertrude Lady Pembroke did not like the portrait. Richmond ends the letter by saying 'one cannot put warm hearts into corpses'.
By cutting down this poor painting, a table covered in books and papers, the knees, and lower half of the overcoat were removed.

76. GERTRUDE, COUNTESS OF PEMBROKE (1840–1906)

Canvas, 30×25 in. (Cut down from 62×39 in.)

Standing, nearly full face, the head, with red hair, slightly looking up, she wears a white satin dress, very low-cut, with an Elizabethan lace collar, puffed sleeves to the elbow, the arms down by her side.

For details of Lady Pembroke, see No. 75.

Provenance: Presumably commissioned by George, 13th Earl of Pembroke, and painted shortly after their marriage in 1874.

Samuel Scott

1702–1772

Born in London, where he painted views and marine scenes. He was a friend of Hogarth and Lambert. Towards the end of his life he retired to Bath, where he died.

77. LINCOLN'S INN FIELDS   *Plate* 124

Canvas, 44×100 in.

Three sides of the Square are shown, as completed

by the middle of the eighteenth century; Lincoln's Inn was first laid out and developed in the first half of the seventeenth century.

Re-lined, cleaned and repaired in 1932. Blisters laid in 1953. In good condition.

Provenance: In the collection before 1774 (Richardson catalogue); probably bought by Henry, 9th Earl of Pembroke (the Architect Earl), before 1750.

78. COVENT GARDEN   *Plate* 125

Canvas, 44 × 100 in.

The north and east sides of the old market are shown; the arcaded houses, designed by Inigo Jones about 1640, were constructed on building leases from the Earl of Bedford. On the left is seen St Paul's Church by Inigo Jones.

Relined and cleaned in 1932 and in 1967. Slight damage in the centre, otherwise in good condition.

Provenance: As No. 77.

79. ENGAGEMENT BETWEEN THE SLOOP H.M.S. 'BLAST' AND TWO SPANISH PRIVATEERS, 1745
Plate 126

Canvas, 32 × 52 in.

The British man-of-war is being attacked in a calm by the two smaller Spanish ships.

Signed: On a piece of driftwood in the left foreground above the letters 'ment' of 'engagement': S. Scott. 1747.

The name 'Blast' was first used under King William III for a bomb vessel; the 'Bombs' were a small class ship, armed with mortars and employed for the bombardment of enemy towns. Sometimes the mortars were removed and the vessels were re-armed with guns; they were then rated as sloops (Admiralty Librarian, 1945).

Cleaned and repaired in 1952. In good condition.

Provenance: Collection Earl of Sandwich; Leggatt Bros.; Sir Sidney Herbert, Bt., who bought it for £525, and on whose death in 1939 it passed into the Wilton Collection.

Sir Winston Spencer-Churchill, K.G., O.M., C.H., Honorary Royal Academician
1874–1965

Statesman, soldier, author, landscape painter.

80. THE PALLADIAN BRIDGE, WILTON

Canvas, 24½ × 19½ in.

Looking upstream at the stone bridge, which was built in 1737.

Painted during one of his many Whitsuntide visits to Wilton between 1920 and 1930.

Provenance: Presented to Lord Pembroke by Lady Churchill in July, 1966.

Robert Thorburn
1815–1885

Born at Dumfries, Scotland; entered the Edinburgh Academy School, and then studied at the Royal Academy, London, in 1836. He was made an A.R.A. in 1848. He was a popular portrait painter in miniature.

81. THE HON. MRS SIDNEY HERBERT (LATER LADY HERBERT OF LEA) AND HER TWO ELDEST CHILDREN, MARY AND GEORGE

Cardboard, laid on wood, 17¾ × 13¼ in. (Arched top.) Miniature style on a large scale.

Seated in a brown dress with white top and sleeves, she holds the naked George on her lap with Mary standing in a white frock which has no top to it, on her right. Next to her is an urn in front of a table covered with a red cloth, on which is a vase of flowers. Background of a brown velvet curtain with a landscape on the right.

Elizabeth A'Court, daughter of General Charles A'Court, and niece of Lord Heytesbury, married in 1846 the Hon. Sidney Herbert, second son of George, 11th Earl of Pembroke, by his second wife, Catherine Woronzow. He was created Baron Herbert of Lea in 1861, dying that same year, nine months before his half-brother Robert, 12th Earl of Pembroke, who was succeeded by the baby George in this painting. Elizabeth Herbert died in 1911 aged 90.

Provenance: Commissioned by the Hon. Sidney Herbert.

Henry T. Wells
1828–1903

Born in London; miniature painter up to 1861, thereafter a popular portrait painter. Elected Royal Academician in 1870.

82. SIDNEY, 14TH EARL OF PEMBROKE, G.C.V.O. (1853–1913)

Canvas, 41 × 33 in.

Standing, full face, wearing a black coat, waistcoat and trousers, high white collar, bow tie, and a fur-lined overcoat; the gloved left hand holds the other glove, the arm resting on a pedestal. Originally the size was 60 × 40 in., but in 1965 this was reduced to its present dimensions, eliminating the signature 'Henry T. Wells, 1898'.

Second son of the Hon. Sidney Herbert (Lord Herbert of Lea) and Elizabeth A'Court; M.P. for Wilton 1877–85, and for Croydon 1886–95, when he succeeded his eldest brother. Lord Steward to Queen Victoria and King Edward VII, 1895–1905. Married in 1877 Lady Beatrix Lambton, eldest daughter of the 2nd Earl of Durham, by whom he had two sons and two daughters.

Provenance: Commissioned by Lord Pembroke.

Richard Wilson
1714–1782

Born at Pengoes in Wales, and moved to Mold; he became a pupil of Thomas Wright in 1729, painting portraits. In 1749 he went to Italy, working in Rome, Venice, Naples, etc. On his return to England he soon became a popular landscape painter, and he was a foundation member of the Royal Academy. He was considerably influenced by Claude Lorraine and Gaspar Dughet.

83. WILTON HOUSE FROM THE SOUTH EAST
Plate 22

Canvas, 39½ × 57½ in.

The house and 'Palladian' bridge are seen across the river Nadder, under a hot summer sky; a group of three figures, one of which is sketching, is by the river bank in the foreground. One man leans on a spade, and the woman holds a parasol. Two other men are further to the left, lying and sitting on the ground, gazing into the water. Near them are two large trees, on one of which is the signature RW (R reversed) in monogram.

Re-lined and cleaned in 1939. In very good condition.

Provenance: Commissioned by Henry, 10th Earl of Pembroke, 1758–60.

Versions: A sketch for this painting (No. 84) in the Wilton collection, with slight variations.

Paul Mellon Collection (Virginia Museum of Fine Arts, 1963), unfinished. Canvas, 39 × 56¾ in. Originally the property of Benjamin Booth (1732–1807). Exhibited at the R.A. Winter Exhibition, 1964–5. Lit.: W. G. Constable, *Richard Wilson and his circle*, 1953, pp. 188–9.

At Highfields, Berkshire, the property of Major R. Dent. 1964. Constable considers this one of four versions; originally the property of the Rev. Scott Trimmer, executor of Turner.

Literature: W. G. Constable, *Richard Wilson and his circle*, 1953, pp. 87–8. Plate 58B

Exhibited: British Institution, 1814; City Art Gallery, Birmingham, 'Richard Wilson and his circle', November, 1948–January, 1949, and at the Tate Gallery, January, 1949.

84. WILTON HOUSE FROM THE SOUTH EAST

Canvas, 13 × 20¼ in.

The house and 'Palladian' Bridge are seen across the river Nadder under a hot summer's sky; a group of three figures, one of which is sketching, is seen by the river bank in the right foreground.

Cleaned in 1935. In very good condition.

Provenance: Commissioned by Henry, 10th Earl of Pembroke, 1758–60. This is a preliminary oil sketch for the larger painting, No. 83, but with variations, including the omission of the two other figures which occur to the left in No. 83.

Literature: W. G. Constable, *Richard Wilson*, p. 188. A charcoal drawing by Wilson which is very similar to this sketch, and is reproduced by Constable as plate 58A, is now in the Leeds City Art Galleries.

85. WILTON HOUSE, SOUTH VIEW FROM THE GARDEN
Plate 23

Canvas, 39¼ × 49 in.

Part of the south front is seen on the left; on the right is the 'Palladian' bridge, and in the distance is the spire of Salisbury Cathedral. Figures are standing about a cedar tree in the foreground, and others are seated on the lawn.

Signed on the tree; RW in monogram (R reversed).

Relined on two canvases, cleaned and repaired in 1935. In good condition.

Provenance: Commissioned by Henry, 10th Earl of Pembroke, 1758–60.

Exhibited: As No. 83.

Literature: As No. 83 (Plate 59A).

86. WILTON HOUSE: VIEW FROM THE HOUSE LOOKING SOUTH ACROSS THE RIVER NADDER

Canvas, $39\frac{1}{4} \times 48$ in.

In the foreground is a group of figures by the river, one of whom is fishing. At the top of the hill on the left is a triumphal arch; to the right is the little classical 'temple' or 'folly' by Sir William Chambers, in the copse on the hill, while lower down to the right are the old seventeenth-century stables.

Cleaned and repaired in 1935. In good condition.

Provenance: Commissioned by Henry, 10th Earl of Pembroke, 1758–60.

Exhibited: As No. 83.

Literature: As No. 83 (Plate 59B).

87. WILTON HOUSE FROM THE SOUTH

Canvas, $39 \times 57\frac{1}{2}$ in.

Painted from the top of the hill in the park, south of the house. Part of the south front is seen to the left; to the right is the 'Palladian' bridge, and beyond it in the distance is Salisbury Cathedral. On the hill in the background is a tented military camp. Three figures are in the foreground, one holding a spade and a jug, the second, a woman, is seated beside a picnic meal, with a child behind her, and a dog.
Signed: RW in monogram (R reversed).

Relined, cleaned in 1935. In very good condition.

Provenance: Commissioned by Henry, 10th Earl of Pembroke, 1758–60.

Exhibited: As No. 83.

Literature: As No. 83 (Plate 60A).

88. WILTON HOUSE, EAST VIEW

Canvas, $38\frac{3}{4} \times 57$ in.

The house is seen at the end of a canal on the right and in the foreground, beside which are figures, and on the left, lined by trees, is the old approach road, on which are carriages.

Signed on a log in the centre foreground: RW in monogram (R reversed).

Relined and cleaned in 1932 and in 1967. Slight

damage in the centre, otherwise in good condition.

Provenance: Commissioned by Henry, 10th Earl of Pembroke, 1758–60.

Exhibited: As No. 83.

Literature: As No. 83 (Plate 60B).

89. THE TOMB OF THE HORATII AND CURATII
Plate 127

Canvas, $18\frac{3}{4} \times 28\frac{1}{4}$ in.

The tomb, which is on the Via Appia Nuova just beyond Albano on the way to Ariccia, stands on sandy ground; a goatherd with goats in the foreground, and there are trees behind the tomb and in the background.

Unsigned. On the back of the canvas is painted in black letters in a late eighteenth- or early nineteenth-century hand 'Pembroke House. Wilson. Tomb of the Horatii and Curatii'.

This refers to the location of the painting at that time, and it is fair to assume that it was bought by Henry, 10th Earl of Pembroke (died 1794) or his son George (died 1827).

Cleaned, blisters secured, and repaired in 1936 and 1962. In very good condition.

Exhibited: Birmingham and London, 1948–9.

Literature: As No. 83 (Plate 82B and pp. 203–4, in which versions are recorded).

90. ARICCIA: A FALLEN TREE

Canvas, $18\frac{3}{4} \times 28\frac{3}{4}$ in.

A tree trunk across a stream, beside which a drover herds his goats. Buildings are seen in the wooded background.

Signed: On the milestone, left foreground: RW in monogram (R reversed).

Cleaned in 1936 and 1965. In very good condition.

Provenance: Probably bought by Henry, 10th Earl of Pembroke.

Exhibited: Birmingham and London, 1948–9.

Literature: As No. 83 (Plate 68B, p. 194).

91. ARICCIA: A FALLEN TREE
Plate 128

Canvas, $18\frac{3}{4} \times 28\frac{3}{4}$ in.

A 'close-up' of the same tree as above, with a wooded background.

Signed: On the trunk of the upright tree RW in monogram (R reversed).

Cleaned, blisters secured, repaired in 1936. In good condition.

Provenance: As No. 90.

Exhibition: Birmingham and London, 1948–9.

Literature: As No. 83.

Richardson in his catalogue (1774) mentions a 'Landscape by Wilson', which could be any of the above three.

John Wootton
? 1686–1764

Landscape and animal painter; a pupil of Jan Wijck.

92. A DOG

Canvas, 32×43 in.

A brown spaniel, seated, with his head turned to the left, and a dead partridge lying at his front feet. A tree is on the left with a landscape and sky in the background.

Cleaned in 1966.

Provenance: In the 1774 catalogue by Richardson, p. 88, is the entry: 'A favourite Dog, by Wotton.', which is the only reason for an attribution to Wootton. It is not signed or dated, but the catalogue was made within nine years of Wootton's death, and in the lifetime of the 10th Earl of Pembroke, by whom it was presumably commissioned. It is not a very good example of Wootton's work.

Johann Zoffany
1734–1810

Born in Frankfurt-am-Main; he became a pupil of Martin Speer at Ratisbon. After twice visiting Rome, he arrived in England about 1761, and soon became a popular painter of portraits, conversation pieces and theatrical subjects.

93. NORTH LUDLOW BERNARD (1705–1766)
Plate 132

Canvas, 29½×24½ in.

Full length, standing in a room, his head turned slightly to his left, wearing a scarlet tunic, buff waistcoat and breeches and black jackboots. A crimson sash is over his left shoulder, and his left hand rests on his sword belt, while his gloved right hand holds the other glove. A three-cornered hat is on a chair near a table on the right, and on the floor in the lower left foreground are a saddle, bridle and stirrups. Above is a large window, and a map and an engraving hang on the back wall.

Cleaned and repaired in 1936. In very good condition.

Bernard entered the Army as a Cornet in the Life Guards, and later exchanged into the Dragoon Guards, reaching the rank of Major. He married in 1751 as her second husband, Mary Fitzwilliam, Countess of Pembroke, widow of Henry, 9th Earl.

Provenance: This portrait, which must have been painted during the five years between Zoffany's arrival in England and Bernard's death in 1766, was in the Fitzwilliam collection at Mount Merrion, Dublin, and brought to Wilton when that house was sold in 1918. It has not previously been recorded.

British School, XVII Century

94. PHILIP, 4TH EARL OF PEMBROKE, K.G. (1584–1649)

Canvas, 33×26 in.

Head and shoulders, in feigned oval, nearly full face, turned slightly to the left, brown hair, beard and moustache, he wears over his black dress with white slashed sleeves, a wide lace collar, under which is the pale blue ribbon of the Garter, from which is suspended an ornament, and a jewelled miniature or order hangs from his neck.

For details of the 4th Earl, see No. 160.

Cleaned in 1952.

Provenance: There is no record of the acquisition of this portrait, which appears to be a seventeenth-century copy of the full-length ascribed to Van Dyck at Longleat.

British School, XVII Century

95. ANNE CLIFFORD, COUNTESS OF PEMBROKE (1589–1675)

Canvas, 21¼×18¼ in.

Head and shoulders, turned slightly to the left; her

brown hair falls in ringlets over her neck, round which she wears a single row of pearls. Her low-cut black dress is edged with white, and a miniature of her first husband, the Earl of Dorset, is shown at the top of the dress. Behind her is a brown column, with a small view of a landscape with a tree on the left.

Cleaned and old re-paints removed in 1950. In fair condition.

Anne Clifford was the eldest daughter of George Clifford, 3rd Earl of Cumberland, and Lady Margaret Russell, youngest daughter of Francis, 2nd Earl of Bedford. She married first, in 1609, Richard Sackville, 3rd Earl of Dorset (died 1624), by whom she had two sons and two daughters. The sons died young. In 1630 she married Philip, 1st Earl of Montgomery and 4th Earl of Pembroke, and is seen seated on his left in the great Van Dyck family group (No. 158). Her second marriage, which was childless, was not a very happy one, and in the 1640s she left Wilton and retired to her vast possessions and numerous castles in Cumberland and Westmorland (Appleby, Brough, Skipton and others), where she spent the remainder of her life, defying Cromwell in the Civil War, and rebuilding some of the castles he had destroyed.

Provenance: There is no record of when this portrait, which is neither good nor flattering, was acquired, but judging from her age, it may have been painted after her first husband's death, and before her re-marriage.

Across the top left-hand corner is painted 'Ann, Countess of Dorset, afterwards Countess of Pembroke, with a miniature of the Earl of Dorset. Died. 1675.'

There are portraits of her at Knole, Castle Ashby, formerly at Appleby, and Dulwich, and in the National Portrait Gallery (No. 402), half length, as an old lady.

British School, XVII Century

96. PORTRAIT OF AN UNKNOWN WOMAN

Wood, 35×27 in.

Three-quarter length, facing, wearing a black dress with white lace ruff, and cuffs and cap. In her right hand she holds a red-bound book, and her left arm rests against her dress. There are rings on both her thumbs. A high-backed chair is behind to her right, and a green curtain on the left.

Cleaned, old re-paints removed, and repaired in 1950.

Provenance: There is no mention of this painting in the eighteenth-century catalogues; Wilkinson included it in his, without examining the obviously false inscription in the top left-hand corner which came away easily when it was being cleaned, as did quite a lot of the face and hair. Nor did he compare it with the engravings of Mary Sidney, Countess of Pembroke, as a young and middle-aged woman, which show her to have had a long face unlike the face in this portrait. Some unscrupulous dealer 'dolled' up a painting, and added the inscription, 'Mary Sidney, Countess of Pembroke' in the first half of the nineteenth century and sold it to a member of the family, who, as there was no portrait of her at Wilton (the 1647 fire almost certainly burnt what family paintings there were in the house at the time) fell into the trap.

It has proved impossible to identify the sitter or the artist.

British School, XVII Century

97. MARGARET SAWYER, COUNTESS OF PEM-BROKE (?1660–1706)

Canvas, 50×40 in.

Three-quarter length, standing, full face, her long hair falling over her shoulders; she wears a blue satin dress with a white bodice, and sleeves at the elbow, her left arm bent and holding her dress in front, with the right arm extended down her side. Dark background, with part of a tree on the right.

Cleaned in 1960.

For details of Margaret, Countess of Pembroke, see No. 129.

Provenance: Commissioned by Thomas, 8th Earl of Pembroke; it is impossible to give any attribution with certainty, but it is similar to portraits by Kneller, and she appears to be about the same age as in the Van der Vaart portrait (No. 129), which is dated 1687.

British School, XVIII Century

98. PORTRAIT OF A YOUNG WOMAN

Canvas, 29×24 in.

Standing, nearly full face, the body turned to the

left, a blue bow in brown hair in ringlets, a pearl necklace and ear-rings, and a pearl brooch on her white satin dress, trimmed with lace. Over her left shoulder is a blue drapery, which floats behind her; with the index finger of her right hand and her arm extended, she points at some object at which a brown and white spaniel is looking. Faint background of trees and shrubs.

Cleaned in 1960.

This young woman cannot be identified as any member of the Herbert family; the date could be about 1740, though she is dressed in seventeenth-century clothes – a form of fancy dress – which was sometimes adopted in the eighteenth century.

Provenance: Not traced in any previous catalogue; probably bought or commissioned by the 9th or the 10th Earl.

99. PORTRAIT OF A YOUNG WOMAN

Canvas, $18 \times 14\frac{1}{2}$ in.

Standing, three-quarter length, her head inclined to the left. She wears a large white hat lined with red, tilted to one side and tied under her chin with a blue bow. She has a pale yellow coat with green cuffs, a yellow skirt, and a red and white bodice, covered by a transparent white drapery. Her left arm is extended and she holds a rake; her right arm rests on a stone plinth, on which is a small basket of flowers, and she holds some flowers in her hand. Background of an arch, red drapery and sky.

Cleaned in 1960.

The unknown young woman in country clothes has not been identified; it may have been an imaginative composition or a sketch for some larger picture.

Provenance: Not traced in any previous catalogue; probably bought in the eighteenth or nineteenth century.

Early XIX Century Copy
after Nathaniel Hone
1717-1784

Born in Dublin; moved to London about 1750. He was one of the foundation members of the Royal Academy. He was a popular portrait and miniature painter.

100. RICHARD, 7TH VISCOUNT FITZWILLIAM (1745-1816)

Canvas, $29\frac{1}{4} \times 24$ in.

Head and shoulders, seated, full face, with white wig or powdered hair, wearing a white cravat and brown coat edged with gold braid. His left arm is crossed in front, resting on a book on a table, the left hand just showing above the right hand.

Cleaned in 1960.

Lord Fitzwilliam was the eldest son of the 6th Viscount and Catherine Decker, eldest daughter of Sir Mathew Decker, Bt., a Dutchman who settled in England in 1702 and was created a Baronet by George I. The Irish family of Fitzwilliam had owned property in and around Dublin since the twelfth century; in 1629 Charles I created Thomas Fitzwilliam of Merrion, Co. Dublin, the first Viscount. The 7th Viscount never married, and his brothers died without children, so that the title died out. When Richard Fitzwilliam died in 1816, he founded the Fitzwilliam Museum at Cambridge, leaving half the contents of his house at Richmond, where he mainly lived, to the Museum, and the remainder, as well as the Irish house, Mount Merrion, and the Dublin Estate, to his cousin, George, 11th Earl of Pembroke, whose grandmother was a sister of the 6th Viscount.

Provenance: From Mount Merrion, Co. Dublin, to George, 11th Earl of Pembroke.

The original portrait by Hone is in the possession of Mr Verschoyle-Campbell (1965) in Ireland.

British School, XVIII Century

100A. THE THREE SONS OF THE 6TH VISCOUNT FITZWILLIAM

Canvas, $73 \times 57\frac{3}{4}$ in.

The eldest, standing, full face, in the centre, wears a black three-cornered hat, a white lace frill round his neck, above a grey coat, which reaches to his knees and is open to show a white waistcoat, green breeches and stockings, black shoes with silver buckles. He holds a top in his left hand, with the string in his right. To the right, similarly dressed, but in dark blue, with his right knee on the ground, his left hand on his left knee, is the second son, who holds a top in the palm of his right hand, watching it spin. Behind him stands the youngest son, holding a

black hat in his left hand, and pointing behind his
kneeling brother's head with his right. Background
of a high stone wall lined with trees on the right and
a landscape and sky on the left.

Cleaned in 1966. A very faint and indecipherable
signature and date at the extreme edge at the base
of the painting near the left corner appears to begin
with the letters Ro–p— and the date 1759; so far
it has not been possible to make any definite attribution. Professor Waterhouse has seen photographs
and says that it is painted in the Hayman tradition.
It may be by an obscure Irish painter.

Richard, 7th Viscount Fitzwilliam, 1745–1816 (see
No. 100), John, 1752–1830, who died unmarried,
and Thomas, 1755–1833, who married in 1780, but
died without children when the title became extinct,
were the sons of the 6th Viscount and Catherine,
eldest daughter of Sir Mathew Decker, Bt.

Provenance: Probably painted for the 6th Viscount,
it hung in his Irish house, Mount Merrion, Co.
Dublin, and when that house was sold in 1918, was
brought from there to Wilton.

British School, Late XIX Century

101. GEORGE, 13TH EARL OF PEMBROKE (1850–
1895)

Pastel on canvas, 52×30 in.

Three-quarter length, standing, holding a boat-hook
in his right hand, his head turned to the left. He wears
an open-neck pink and white striped shirt, brown
tweed coat and white trousers.

For details of George, Lord Pembroke, see No. 75.

Provenance: Commissioned by the sitter.

DUTCH SCHOOL

Nicolaes Berchem
1620–1683

Son of Pieter Claesz; adopted the name of Berchem. He studied with his father, then with Jan van Goyen and others. After visiting Italy, he returned to work in Haarlem, and later in Amsterdam.

102. LANDSCAPE WITH FIGURES AND ANIMALS

Canvas on wood, 18×24 in.

On the left a man rides a donkey, beside which is a dog; on the right is another man with three cows and a sheep, and behind them a wood. Background of rolling country and sky.

Cleaned in 1934 and 1951. In good condition.

Provenance: At Wilton before 1730. Probably bought by Thomas, 8th Earl of Pembroke.

Abraham Bloemaert
1564–1651

Born at Gorcum; son of an architect and sculptor, studied under Frans Floris and others. Visited Paris, worked mainly in Amsterdam and Utrecht. Painted a variety of subjects, allegorical and historical, and landscapes, flowers, and animals.

103. SHEPHERD AND SHEPHERDESS   *Plate 67*

Canvas, 38×48 in.

A girl sits, left centre, wearing a large sun hat and a buff-coloured dress; she holds on her lap a brass bowl. On the right, reclining against a rock, is a half-naked shepherd, gazing up at her. In the background is a lake or the sea.

Cleaned in 1930. In good condition.

Provenance: At Wilton before 1730; probably bought by Thomas, 8th Earl of Pembroke.

Exhibited: Royal Academy '17th Century Art in Europe', 1938, No. 152.

Gerard Ter Borch
1617–1681

Born at Zwolle, studied under his father and Pieter Molijn; visited England, Germany, France, Italy, and Spain. Famous for his small portraits and 'conversation' scenes.

104. BATTLE SCENE   *Plate 72*

Copper, 10×12 in.

On the left is a group of some ten horsemen in armour with spears, who are attacking, centre, a soldier on a white horse, which has fallen. To the right are three figures holding muskets, looking on.

Cleaned, loose paint secured, and repaired in 1947. In good condition.

Provenance: Woronzow collection. Left by Count Simon Woronzow to his daughter, Catherine, Countess of Pembroke (d. 1856); the frame bears her seal. On the back of the picture is written: 'By a famous Master of the Dutch School whose name is unknown.'

The discovery of this very early example (about 1635) of Ter Borch's work is due to Dr S. J. Gudlaugsson, Curator of the Rijksbureau voor Kunsthistorische Documentatie, The Hague, and Professor I. Q. van Regteren Altena, who visited Wilton in 1951.

In the Wilkinson catalogue, No. 249, Flemish School.

Richard Brakenburgh
1650–1702

Born and died at Haarlem.

105. INTERIOR OF A SCHOOL   *Plate 70*

Canvas, 34½×47 in.

An elderly schoolmaster, seated behind a desk, wears a black hat, with a white collar on a black and brown dress; his left hand holds some form of instrument or ruler and rests on the desk; his right hand is out-stretched and points to a child writing. About twenty-five boys and girls, some studying, some laughing and playing about, are standing or sitting all around him. A dog is in the lower left fore-ground. A wicker basket hangs from the wall behind the schoolmaster, and books, baskets, and other objects are on the floor or on tables.

Cleaned and re-paints removed in 1950.

Provenance: At Wilton before 1730, probably bought by Thomas, 8th Earl of Pembroke.

Gambarini, p. 78, describes what must be this picture under the heading of: 'Gonsales, of a Span-ish Family settled in Flanders; he was commonly called little Van Dyck from painting little figures in great perspective; it is of children at a Flemish School.'

Jan Ten Compe
1713–1761

A pupil of Dirk Dalens and follower of Jan van der Heyden.

106. ALMSHOUSES ON THE RIVER AMSTEL, AMSTERDAM   *Plate* 79

Canvas, 23 × 17¾ in.

The brick almshouses face the river on the right; in the centre, two white horses pulling a cart are crossing a bridge, which spans a canal. To the left are more houses, with people walking and riding between them and the river, which has a number of boats on it.

Cleaned in 1939 and 1958. In very good condition.

Provenance: Leggatt Bros.; Sir Sidney Herbert, Bt., on whose death in 1939 it came to Wilton.

School of Frans Hals
1580–1666

Hals was probably born in Antwerp, but his parents had settled in Haarlem by 1591, and it was there that he lived and died.

107. A MAN AMUSING CHILDREN WITH A RUMMEL POT   *Plate* 68

Canvas, 43 × 34 in.

The laughing man, dressed in a black coat and wear-ing an old black hat, holds the musical instrument known as a rummel pot with both hands. He is surrounded by six children of different ages, all laughing.

Relined, and cleaned in 1930. In good condition.

Pentimenti in the top right-hand corner: three additional faces painted out, and in the top left-hand corner one face, all of older people. These were invisible before cleaning.

Provenance: At Wilton before 1730; probably bought by Thomas, 8th Earl of Pembroke.

Literature and Versions: Hofstede de Groot (*Catalogue Raisonné*, Vol. III, 1910, No. 137) enumerates fifteen versions, and considers the Wilton painting the sixth.

Valentiner (*Klassiker der Kunst, Frans Hals*, 1923), reproduces the Cook and Wilton versions, and considers the Cook version the closest to the lost original.

More recently N. S. Trivas (*The Paintings of Frans Hals*, Phaidon Press, 1941) in Appendix 4 states that more than twenty versions are known, including that in the Art Institute of Chicago (ex C. H. Worcester), and some years ago versions were sold in Paris (Marny), New York (Bacon), Berlin, and more recently at Christie's (Dec. 19, 1938, and March 13, 1939, lots 64 and 74). All the versions vary in composition.

Perhaps the Wilton version is by Judith Leyster, (1609–1660), a pupil of Hals, and wife of Jan Molenaer.

Adriaen Hanneman
1601–1671

Portrait painter; he was a pupil of Jan van Ravesteyn, and a follower of Van Dyck. Charles I invited him to England, where he spent sixteen years, receiving many commissions, before returning to Holland.

108. SIR EDWARD NICHOLAS (1593–1669)

Canvas, 32 × 26 in.

Half length, turned slightly to the right. On his head, he wears a black skull-cap partially covering his white hair, which falls over his neck; he has a white moustache and small 'imperial' beard. His black dress or cape is tied with a silver ribbon below a square-cut collar.

Cleaned and repaired in 1950. The painting has suffered considerable damage in the past, three holes having been made in the canvas, on the right.

Sir Edward Nicholas was Secretary of State to Charles I and Charles II. His father, John, was employed by the Pembroke family at Wilton, and lived not far away at Winterbourne Earls; Sir Edward's son, Sir John, represented Wilton in the 1660 Parliament with T. Mompesson.

Provenance: Commissioned or bought by the 4th or 5th Lord Pembroke.

Version: The original of this painting, of which the Wilton example is a duplicate or copy, is in the possession of the Earl of Crawford and Balcarres, who is a descendant of Sir Edward Nicholas.

G. Van Heckell

A little-known painter of the seventeenth century.

109. PEASANTS IN A FARM HOUSE

Wood, 11 × 14½ in.

A bearded man stands behind his family; at his feet sits his daughter holding a bowl and a spoon, and asleep in a chair is his wife, wearing a red blouse, brown skirt, and white apron. A baby is sleeping in a cradle on her left, and a cat sits on the lower half of a small door or window, which is half open.

Signed, very faintly, between the cradle and the edge of the panel: G. v. Heckell. 1660.

Repaired and cleaned in 1936 and 1958.

Provenance: At Wilton before 1730; attributed by Gambarini to Brouwer, p. 76, and by Wilkinson to his school (288).

Egbert van Heemskerk, the Elder
1610–1680

Born in Haarlem, he soon became well known for his interiors of taverns and schools and farm houses.

110. INTERIOR OF A FARM HOUSE   *Plate* 64

Wood, 15¼ × 19½ in.

Four peasants are seated at a table, playing back-

gammon or draughts, while two more stand near; another is dimly seen behind an open door. To the right, standing at a table, is a woman cutting bread or cheese, and below her is a small girl in a red dress holding a hat.

Signed, on the central table leg: E. Kerch. 1677.

Cleaned and repaired in 1936 and 1963. In good condition.

Provenance: At Wilton before 1730; probably bought by Thomas, 8th Earl of Pembroke.

Jan van der Heyden
1637–1712

Lived and worked in Amsterdam.

III. THE CHURCH OF ST MICHAEL, ANTWERP
Plate 78

Wood, 19½ × 27 in.

The church is seen at the back of the cobbled courtyard, enclosed by brick walls, and two lines of trees, left and right, run the length of the courtyard. Right foreground is a woman, left foreground a child; a white-robed priest and a man with a dog are in the centre walking towards the church, from which four white-robed priests, one carrying a cross, are emerging.

In 1933 this picture was found, unframed and very badly damaged, in a drawer of a table in the house; the principal damages were on the right in the brick wall and the foliage of the trees, and some of the paint had flaked off the roof and walls of the church. Owing to the minute details of the painting of every brick and leaf, stone, slates, and cobbles, it was impossible to do more than fill in with plain colours the patches where the paint was missing altogether, after the picture had been cleaned and the loose paint secured. The picture had once been a fine example of Van der Heyden's work, but to describe it as a complete wreck, as Wilkinson did, was an overstatement. In the 1827 inventory it was described as 'much damaged'.

Provenance: At Wilton before 1730, probably bought by Thomas, 8th Earl of Pembroke.

Gerrit van Honthorst
1590–1656

Born in Utrecht; studied under Abraham Bloemaert. He went to Rome about 1610, where he became well known for his religious pictures, his portraits, and the frescoes in the Church of S. Maria della Scala. After about ten years he returned to Holland, where he became Dean of the Guild of St Luke. The Queen of Bohemia patronized him, and told her brother Charles I of England about him; he arrived in London in 1628, and received commissions from the King and members of his Court; he decorated parts of Whitehall Palace. On returning to Holland, he painted frescoes in The Hague and Ryswyck, as well as continuing to paint portraits.

112. PRINCE RUPERT (1619–1682)   *Plate 65*
Wood, 30 × 23½ in.

Head and shoulders, turned slightly to the right, in a feigned oval. He wears a dark silver-grey dress with slashed sleeves, and an elaborate white lace collar, and a large black hat.

Cleaned, cracks secured, and repaired in 1936.

Prince Rupert of the Rhine was the third son of James I's daughter, Elizabeth, and Frederick, King of Bohemia. Prince Rupert came to England in 1635 to join his brother Charles Louis at the court of their uncle, Charles I, for whom he fought with distinction in the Civil War, commanding the cavalry. This portrait was probably painted in the year he arrived or in 1636, when he was sixteen.

Provenance: At Wilton before 1730; probably purchased in the seventeenth century by Philip, 4th Earl of Pembroke, or commissioned by him, or given to him by the King.

Exhibited: Royal Academy, *Seventeenth Century Art in Europe*, 1938, No. 151, and reproduced.

113. PRINCESS SOPHIA OF BOHEMIA (1630–1714)
                                        Plate 66
Canvas, 21 × 18½ in.

Head and shoulders, leaning forward to the left; her left hand holds a rose, her right hand a crook. She wears a buff-coloured dress and a broad-rimmed black hat; she represents a shepherdess.

Cleaned and repaired in 1930. In good condition.

Princess Sophia was the fifth daughter of the Elector Palatine of the Rhine, King of Bohemia, and Elizabeth, sister of Charles I of England. She married in 1658 Ernest Augustus, Duke of Brunswick, Elector of Hanover, and was the mother of George I of England.

Probably painted in 1643, when Princess Sophia was thirteen years old.

Provenance: Mentioned in Van der Doort's Catalogue of Charles I's pictures as hanging in the Queen's little dressing-room at Whitehall Palace (Walpole Society, Vol. XXXVII, 1958–60. Van der Doort, p. 176). Probably acquired by Philip, 5th Earl, or Thomas, 8th Earl of Pembroke in the seventeenth century. (See the note under No. 169, 'bought of the Earl of Peterborough'.)

Leonard Knyff
1650–1722

Born in The Hague, settled in England in 1681.

114. TOPOGRAPHICAL VIEW OF WILTON
Canvas, 38½ × 53 in.

The top half of the picture shows the house, gardens, park, and surrounding countryside as if from the air. The lower half is divided into small sections; on the left is the south side of the house, and below it a waterfall and statuary; in the centre are the old De Caus stables and below them the inside of the grotto; on the right is the loggia, with a bowling green in front, and below it the outside of the grotto.

Cleaned and repaired in 1935. Two damages in the centre, one a right-angled tear.

Provenance: Commissioned by Thomas, 8th Earl of Pembroke, and painted about 1700–10.

Pieter van Laer
1592–1642

He left Holland as a young man for Italy, and worked in Rome for many years. He returned to Haarlem in 1638, and died there in 1642. In Italy, he became known as 'Bamboccio' as most of his pictures are of fairs, peasants, children, taverns, and masquerades.

115. A BOY TAKING PHYSIC
Wood, 7¼ × 6 in.

Seated on a rock, turned to the right, a fair-haired

boy, dressed in a red and white smock with short blue trousers, and with bare legs, holds a bowl with his right hand, while a man, standing behind him, wearing a brown hat, garment and leggings, also holds the bowl with his left hand, and in his right hand he holds a whip.

Cleaned in 1947. In good condition.

Provenance: At Wilton before 1730, probably bought by Thomas, 8th Earl of Pembroke.

Lucas van Leyden
? 1494–1533

Born at Leyden, son of Hugo Jacobsz, a painter, under whom he studied; possibly influenced by Dürer, whom he knew, and by Gossaert. His pictures are rare; he died before he was forty.

116. THE CARD PLAYERS   *Plates 37–38*

Wood, 14 × 18 in.

Nine figures, in a variety of brilliantly coloured dresses and hats, are seated at or standing by a card table, which is covered with a green cloth and has coins on it; four of the players hold cards. Through a little window in the centre background green hills and trees are seen.

Blisters secured, and picture repaired and cleaned in 1929; surface cleaned in 1955. In very good condition.

Provenance: At Wilton before 1730, probably bought by Thomas, 8th Earl of Pembroke, who, when he acquired this masterpiece, may not have realized that it was one of the few authentic works by the Master of the School of Leyden. It was painted about 1514, when the artist was little more than twenty years old.

Versions: At Tyninghame (Earl of Haddington), slightly larger, and probably a sixteenth or early seventeenth century copy.

Exhibited: Manchester, 1857, *The Art Treasures of the United Kingdom*, No. 422. Burlington Fine Arts, 1892, No. 59. *Dutch Art*, Royal Academy, 1929, No. 20, Pl. III.

Literature: Waagen, III, 152; N. Beets, 1913, Pl. XXXI; M. J. Friedländer, *Die altniederländische Malerei*, vol. X, p. 137, No. 141; *Dutch Painting*, text by Jean Leymarie (Skira 1956), colour pl. p. 49.

Frans van Mieris
1635–1681

Born at Leyden, son of a goldsmith, he was a pupil of Gerard Dou and others; he painted portraits and genre scenes. He lived and died in Leyden.

117. SELF-PORTRAIT

Copper oval let into a panel, 11 × 9½ in.

Head and shoulders, head turned slightly towards the left, wearing a black dress, seen through an open portal, behind which is a red, green, and gold drapery.

Repaints removed, blisters secured, and cleaned in 1925. This must have once been a brilliant little self-portrait, but at some time the paint on the copper blistered badly, and restoration was crudely carried out, probably in the nineteenth century.

Provenance: On the back of the panel is written 'The head of Mieris by himself; bought by Henry, Earl of Pembroke, 1743'. The 9th Earl died in 1750.

Daniel Mytens
c. 1590–1647

Born at Delft; he came to England in 1618, and Charles I appointed him Court Painter. He continued to work in England after the arrival of Van Dyck, but later returned to Holland, where he died.

118. PHILIP, 4TH EARL OF PEMBROKE AND 1ST EARL OF MONTGOMERY, K.G. (1584–1649)   *Plate 3*

Canvas, 86 × 53 in.

Full length, standing, half turned to his left, wearing a black court dress and cloak, with a white lace collar and cuffs; the Riband and George of the Garter are suspended from his neck, and he wears the Garter below his left knee. The stockings are blue with black shoes with bows. In his right hand he holds his wand of office as Lord Chamberlain, while in his gloved left hand he holds a black hat and the other glove; the hilt of his sword is between his hip and his wrist. In the left background is a red curtain, and in the top right hand corner is a small view through a window of a brick house, which might be the Tudor Ramsbury Manor, near Marlborough, which was owned by the family (and where he lived, when not in London, while his elder brother lived at Wilton) from the middle of the sixteenth until late in the seventeenth century.

Cleaned and blisters secured in 1939. In fair condition.

This is one of the best portraits of the 4th Earl, and a good example of Mytens; it was painted about 1625.

For details of the 4th Earl, see No. 160.

Provenance: Earl of Yarborough; Leggatt Bros.; Sir Sidney Herbert, Bt., who purchased it for £900, and on whose death in 1939 it came to Wilton.

Versions: A very similar version, formerly at Bramshill, Hants (the property of Sir William Cope, Bt.), was sold at Christie's in 1938 for twenty-seven guineas.

119. WILLIAM, 3RD EARL OF PEMBROKE, K.G. (1580–1630)

Canvas, 30 × 25 in.

Half length, the face and body turned slightly to the left, with beard and moustache, and a gold ear-ring in his right ear. He wears a black court dress with a wide lace collar from which falls a lace tassel with a ring attached. The blue ribbon of the Garter, suspended from the neck under the lace collar, has a circular jewelled ornament enclosing a miniature which might be of James I, attached to it. From a gold belt round his waist hangs the gold key of office of Lord Steward of the Household, and the tip of the white wand of office is shown. On his left sleeve is embroidered the Star of the Garter.

Cleaned in 1952. In fair condition.

For details of the 3rd Earl, see No. 159.

Provenance: Probably commissioned by the sitter, and painted about 1625, the same year in which the full length of his brother was painted.

Versions: Identical, three-quarter length by Mytens, the property of the Hon. Robin Neville on loan to the Ministry of Works at Audley End, Essex. Almost identical, but with a different jewel and without the wand of office, the property of Mr Mark Harford, of Little Sodbury Manor, Chipping Sodbury, who was given it by his relative, the Hon. Mrs Arthur Strutt, who was left it by her sister, Baroness Daisy de Brienen, who may have bought it at the sale at Christie's in 1904 for twenty-six guineas (Marquess Townshend Collection). Mr Oliver Millar records (*The Tudor, Stuart, and Early Georgian Pictures in the Royal Collection*, London, 1963, p. 84)

that Charles I possessed a portrait of the 3rd Earl by Mytens which was lost with the other Royal paintings, after his execution, and never recovered; it may be this version.

Identical, Breamore House, Fordingbridge (Sir Westrow Hulse, Bt.).

Engraved: Robertus van Voerst.

School of Daniel Mytens

120. WILLIAM, 3RD EARL OF PEMBROKE, K.G. (1580–1630)

Wood, 16 × 12¼ in.

Head and shoulders, turned slightly to the right, he wears a black dress, with a deep ruff of white lace, under which is suspended the blue ribbon of the Garter with pendant jewel.

Repaired and cleaned in 1939.

For details of the 3rd Earl, see No. 159.

Provenance: There is no mention of this painting in earlier catalogues, perhaps because it was in the London house, or, being very small, hung in a bedroom and so was not seen; it is undoubtedly contemporary, and painted towards the end of the 3rd Earl's life, about 1625.

Caspar Netscher
1639–1684

Born at Heidelberg; studied under Gerard ter Borch, whom he imitated, as well as Metsu and Mieris; he painted portraits and genre pictures. He worked mainly at The Hague, where he died.

121. PORTRAIT OF A MAN   *Plate* 73

Wood, 17¾ × 13½ in.

Seated, half turned to the right, in a chair, wearing a brown dress and cloak, with white band and ruffles; on his head is a skull-cap. Behind is a curtain and part of a picture.

Signed, above his left hand: C. Netscher. f. 1670.

Cleaned in 1938. In very good condition.

Provenance: One of the seven pictures given by General Philip Goldsworthy to George, 11th Earl of Pembroke, at the beginning of the nineteenth century.

Cornelis van Poelenburgh
? 1586–1667

Born in Utrecht. A pupil of Abraham Bloemaert; travelled in Italy and came under the influence of Adam Elsheimer.

122. LANDSCAPE WITH FIGURES   *Plate 71*

Wood, 20½ × 32¼ in.

Groups of half-naked women and satyrs are seen seated on rocks, dancing, and bathing in a stream spanned by a bridge, on which are more figures and donkeys. Below by the water are some cattle. In the background on the left is a ruined castle.

Cleaned in 1950. In good condition.

Provenance: At Wilton before 1730; probably bought by Thomas, 8th Earl of Pembroke. Gambarini, p. 67, 'a dance of nymphs and satyrs', correctly attributes it to 'Polemburg'. Mentioned by Wilkinson in Appendix IV as being hung in Herbert House, Belgrave Square, London, in 1907; returned to Wilton after the death of Lady Herbert of Lea in 1911.

Hendrick Gerritsz Pot
? 1585–1657

Born in Haarlem; studied under Karel van Mander, and influenced by Hals. Visited London in 1632, worked mainly in Haarlem, but died in Amsterdam, where he lived for the last eight or nine years of his life. Painted small portraits and scenes.

123. PHILIP, 4TH EARL OF PEMBROKE, K.G.

Canvas, 26 × 23 in.

Full length, standing, with his right foot on the lower step of a portico, wearing a black court dress, and blue stockings, and underneath the deep white lace collar is suspended the blue ribbon of the Garter, with the Star of the Order embroidered on the black cloak which he holds up with his right hand; his left hand holds his wand of office as Lord Chamberlain to Charles I. Landscape of a balustrade, on which are statues, beyond which are trees and sky.

Cleaned in 1950. In good condition.

For details of the 4th Earl, see No. 160.

Provenance: Commissioned by Lord Pembroke; painted in the late 1630s, and modelled on the full length by Van Dyck.

Previously attributed to the school of Van Dyck, Gonzales Coques, and others. Now attributed by Oliver Millar to Pot, the background possibly by Van Deeren.

At Windsor Castle is a portrait of Charles I by Pot, painted about 1634 in London; the Wilton portrait was no doubt commissioned shortly after.

Rembrandt van Rijn
1606–1669

Born at Leyden, the son of Harmen Gerritsz van Rijn, a miller. He studied first at Leyden, then in Amsterdam, where he lived and died.

124. PORTRAIT OF HIS MOTHER   *Frontispiece*

Canvas, 29¾ × 25 in.

Seated, facing half left, with a large open book on her knees, in a brown dress, with a brown and mauve hood on her head, and wearing pince-nez.

Cleaned in 1933 and 1963. In very good condition.

Neeltgen Willemsdochter van Zuytbroek, wife of Harmen Gerritsz van Rijn, died in September, 1640.

This is probably the first of the portraits Rembrandt painted of his mother, and though not signed or dated, is generally thought to have been done in 1629.

Provenance: Purchased by Thomas, 8th Earl of Pembroke, perhaps as early as 1685, when he was in Holland.

Literature: Bode and Hofstede de Groot, *The Complete Work of Rembrandt*, p. 381, No. 263; Michel, Vol. I, p. 40; Hofstede de Groot, *A Catalogue Raisonné of the Works of the Most Eminent Dutch Painters of the Seventeenth Century*, Vol. VI (London, 1916), p. 320; Valentiner, *Rembrandt: Des Meisters Gemälde*, Klassiker de Kunst (1908), p. 37; Bredius, *The Paintings of Rembrandt* (Phaidon Edition, 1942), p. 68; Borenius, *Rembrandt, Selected Paintings* (Phaidon Press, 1944), p. 29, Pl. 1.

Exhibited: Arts Council, Edinburgh, 1950.

Roelandt Savery
? 1576-1639

Born at Courtrai in Flanders, but went to Amsterdam at an early age; a pupil of his brother Jacob. Worked for the Emperor Rudolf II at Prague, about 1605, and also in Vienna. He returned to Amsterdam in 1613, but moved in 1619 to Utrecht, where he died.

125. ST JOHN PREACHING   *Plate 62*

Copper, $8\frac{1}{4} \times 13\frac{1}{4}$ in.

St John stands with his right arm raised, at the foot of a large tree with a wood behind him, preaching to a group of men and women in a variety of dresses, some biblical, some seventeenth century; two of the men are mounted, and another standing holds a spear. In the lower right foreground a woman is seated with a baby in her arms, and a small child stands beside her with a dog. Behind her is a goat, and walking up the hill two more figures. In the deep shadows of the wood on the left are two figures.

Cleaned in 1960. In good condition.

Provenance: At Wilton before 1730; probably bought by Thomas, 8th Earl of Pembroke.

Godefried Cornelisz Schalcken
1643-1706

Born at Made near Dordrecht, he became a pupil of Samuel van Hoogstraten and afterwards of Dou. He visited England in 1692 and stayed for six years, returned to The Hague, where he lived and died.

126. A YOUNG WOMAN HOLDING A CANDLE

Canvas, $18\frac{1}{2} \times 14\frac{3}{4}$ in.

Head and shoulders; a candle in her left hand lights her face turned slightly to her right; she has black ribbons in her fair hair.

Signed in the right lower corner: G. Schalcken.

Cleaned in 1964. In good condition.

Provenance: At Wilton before 1730; probably bought by Thomas, 8th Earl of Pembroke.

Gerard Soest
? 1600-1681

Probably born in Westphalia; he worked mainly in Holland, and visited England about the middle of the seventeenth century.

127. PORTRAIT OF A YOUNG MAN   *Plate 75*

Canvas, $29 \times 24\frac{1}{4}$ in.

Head and shoulders, turned to the left. Long brown hair falls over the collar of his grey-green dress.

Relined, cleaned and repaired in 1938. In very good condition.

Provenance: It is impossible to trace this portrait in the eighteenth-century catalogues, and Wilkinson's story that it was bought at the 'Slingsby' sale by Lady Herbert of Lea was denied by her in a letter at Wilton (1907).

Attributed in 1937 by Isherwood Kay to Soest; Wilkinson calls it Dobson (No. 215) (who died in 1646), which is clearly wrong. If it is a family portrait, it was presumably commissioned, or it may have been bought sometime in the late eighteenth or early nineteenth century in the knowledge or belief that it was of a member of the Herbert family.

Hendrick van Steenwijck
? 1580-1648

A pupil of his father, who had the same Christian name; he came to England about 1630, and died in London.

128. THE LIBERATION OF ST PETER   *Plate 69*

Wood, $11\frac{1}{2} \times 19\frac{1}{2}$ in.

St Peter is seen with an angel walking through what appear to be the vaults of a church or prison. A figure is seated, left, asleep against a pillar, and some soldiers are asleep in the background.

Blisters secured, repaired and cleaned in 1933. In very good condition.

The Liberation of St Peter was a favourite subject with Steenwijk. Two paintings of it by him are in the Fitzwilliam Museum, Cambridge.

Provenance: At Wilton before 1730; possibly bought at the Lely sale of 1682.

Called Neefs by Wilkinson (95), but attributed by Van Riemsdijk to Steenwijck.

Versions: Windsor Castle; Brunswick Gallery.

Jan van der Vaart

c. 1647–1727

He came to England in 1674, studied under Thomas Wijck, and was later employed by Wissing, whom he followed.

129. MARGARET SAWYER, COUNTESS OF PEMBROKE (? 1660–1706) *Plate 12*

Canvas, 50×40 in.

Seated, facing, wearing a low-cut blue dress, the top edged with white, with white sleeves; her left hand is stroking a lamb which lies on a bank; her right hand holds some kind of food for it. Landscape in the background.

Cleaned in 1936, when the signature 'Jan van der Vaart. 1687.' was revealed above the lamb on the right. Previously attributed to Wissing. In good condition.

Margaret Sawyer was the only daughter of Sir Robert Sawyer, of Highclere, Newbury; in 1684, she married, as his first wife, Thomas, 8th Earl of Pembroke (see No. 134), and they had seven sons and five daughters. She died in 1706.

Another portrait of her is at Petworth, by Michael Dahl, three-quarter length (No. 206, Collins Baker Catalogue).

Provenance: Commissioned by Lord Pembroke three years after his marriage.

Willem van de Velde, the Younger

1633–1707

Son and pupil of William van de Velde the Elder; he also studied under Simon de Vlieger. After working in Holland, he and his father went to London, where they worked under the patronage of Charles II and James II.

130. SHIPPING IN A CALM *Plate 76*

Canvas, 17½×25½ in.

A fishing-boat in the foreground hoists its sail;

further out to sea a three-masted warship fires a gun. Two other warships with sails set are seen and four more lie at anchor.

Signed on a piece of driftwood in the extreme left foreground: W. V. Velde. 1676.

Cleaned in 1935. In very good condition.

Provenance: At Wilton before 1730, probably bought by Thomas, 8th Earl of Pembroke, or it may be one of the two left by General Goldsworthy. (See note on No. 131.)

131. SHIPPING IN A CALM *Plate 77*

Canvas, 16×20 in.

A warship in the right background fires a salute to another at anchor in the left foreground; between them is a small boat full of men rowing. Another boat with two men beside it is beached, as is a larger one in the right foreground. Two more with sails up are seen in the left background.

Signed on a small piece of driftwood in the centre foreground near the beached boat: W. V. V.

Cleaned in 1935. In very good condition.

Provenance: One of the seven pictures given to George, 11th Earl of Pembroke, by General Philip Goldsworthy at the beginning of the nineteenth century.

Note: Catherine, Countess of Pembroke, in a list, dated 1820, of pictures left by Goldsworthy to Lord Pembroke, puts in two Van de Veldes without description; Gambarini in his catalogue of 1731 includes a Calm and a Storm, so that there should be four paintings by this artist at Wilton, whereas there are three.

132. SHIPPING IN A STORM

Canvas, 17½×25½ in.

A fishing-boat with three men sails before the wind, towing a small dinghy; the boat flies a large red and white horizontally striped flag; in the background on the left a large square-rigged ship is seen approaching, and a small fishing-boat is seen in the right background near the shore.

Signed: W. V. Velde.

Cleaned and relined in 1933. In good condition.

Provenance: At Wilton before 1730; probably bought by Thomas, 8th Earl of Pembroke.

Jan Cornelisz Vermeyen
? 1500–1559

Born in Haarlem, studied under his father; visited Italy and Germany. Most of his working life was spent in the Low Countries, and he died in Brussels. He was a friend of Jan van Scorel, whose work is very similar.

133. PORTRAIT OF A MAN   *Plate* 42

Wood, 29½ × 24½ in.

Half length, life size, nearly full face, turned slightly to the right, wearing a fur-lined coat over a red undercoat or waistcoat, a black cap on his head. His left hand holds a piece of paper; his right hand is slightly outstretched, with the index finger pointing. Some draperies behind him are held, left and right, by two stone figures seated on columns.

Cleaned, old repaints removed, and repaired in 1935. In very good condition.

Provenance: First recorded in the 1827 Inventory of Heirlooms at Wilton; Wilkinson records that the painting was presented to George, 11th Earl of Pembroke, by William Eyre, of Newhouse, Salisbury, at the end of the eighteenth century, as a portrait of Sir John More by Holbein.

Literature: Max Friedländer, *Die altniederländische Malerei*, vol. XII, p. 161 and p. 208, No. 391.

Exhibited: Manchester, *The Art Treasures of the United Kingdom*, 1857. No. 51; Tudor Exhibition, 1890, No. 100, as by Holbein.

Willem Wissing
1656–1687

Born in Amsterdam, but worked at The Hague under William Doudyns. He went to France, and then to England, where he became an assistant to Sir Peter Lely. He died at Burghley House.

134. THOMAS, 8TH EARL OF PEMBROKE, K.G.
(1656–1733)   *Plate* 11

Canvas, 53 × 40 in.

Three-quarter length, standing in full armour, face and body turned slightly to his left; his right hand holds a baton, and his left hand a sword. In the background to the left, ships are seen through an arch in the rocks by a tree.

Cleaned and repaired in 1936 and 1964. Below the ship there are pentimenti of one or two people on white horses riding to the left; they are very faint, almost ghost-like. In good condition.

Thomas Herbert was the third son of Philip, 5th Earl of Pembroke, and his second wife, Catherine Villiers, and succeeded his brother, Philip, the 7th Earl, in 1683. He held many high offices of State, including that of Lord High Admiral in 1702 and 1709, the only commoner to do so. In 1700 he was created a Knight of the Garter. Lord Pembroke carried the Sword of State at five Coronations (a record) – those of James II, William and Mary, Anne, George I and George II. In 1684 he married Margaret Sawyer, daughter of Sir Robert Sawyer, of Highclere, Newbury; she died in 1706, having had seven sons and five daughters. In 1708 he married Barbara, widow of Lord Arundel, and daughter of Sir Thomas Slingsby, and by her had one daughter, Barbara. Lady Pembroke died in 1721, and in 1725, Thomas married for the third time, Mary, sister of Viscount Howe.

Lord Pembroke was a collector on the grand scale, employing agents on the continent to acquire paintings, drawings, books, sculpture and coins. The majority of the paintings of the foreign schools were bought by him, and much of the sculpture came from the Mazarin, Arundel and Giustiniani Collections.

Provenance: Commissioned in 1685, when he was commanding British cavalry in Holland, where Wissing was painting Princess Mary and William of Orange by order of James II. This would account for the pentimenti of horses and riders which represented a battle scene; this was altered some fifteen or sixteen years after Wissing's death, by which time Lord Pembroke had received the Garter (1700), which has been added, – the lesser 'George' and part of the Riband – and he had been made Lord High Admiral (1702).

Gambarini, p. 13, says 'it is by Mr Wissing; he did two originals, the other is at London. Mr Smith made a mezzo-tento Print after it'.

Versions: At Somerley Park, Ringwood, Hants (Lord Normanton), which is probably the second original; Thomas, Lord Pembroke's great grand-daughter, Diana, married Lord Normanton in 1816, and perhaps it was given to her as a wedding present. National Maritime Museum, Greenwich (ex Mr D. Minlore), 1939. – Earl Howe, Penn, Bucks. – Mr

N. C. E. Ashton, 30 Addison Road, London (1954). – University of Kansas Museum of Art, 1966. – Clerk (Penicuik), 1955. – The Parker Gallery, 1955. – Wyndham Law, 1935. – Sotheby, 1945.

Professor James Connelly of the Department of Art History at the University of Kansas Museum of Art has kindly supplied the list of versions, and suggested the date and other details of the original.

Engraving: By John Smith.

? Philips Wouwermans
1619–1668

Born in Haarlem, son of a painter, under whom he studied as well as under Jan Wijnants. Painted mainly animals and figures in landscapes.

135. THE DEPARTURE OF THE PRODIGAL SON

Copper, backed with wood, 16 × 19½ in.

The son, in the centre foreground, dressed in white and blue, is being seen off by his father, relations, friends and servants, at the foot of a flight of stone steps on the right. His white horse, held by a groom, paws the ground while a servant loads luggage onto another horse. Dogs and groups of people are seen in the foreground and in the middle distance, where there is a fountain; background of hills, castles, rocks and trees.

Cleaned, blisters secured, and repaired in 1932.

Both this and the companion picture were much damaged; to prevent the thin copper plates bending again, which they had done, thereby causing the paint to flake off, they were backed by panels.

It is to be noted that none of the authentic paintings by Wouwermans in the National Gallery is painted on copper, and it is most likely that these two paintings are by a pupil or imitator.

Provenance: At Wilton before 1730; probably bought by Thomas, 8th Earl of Pembroke.

136. THE RETURN OF THE PRODIGAL SON

Copper, backed with wood, 16 × 19½ in.

The son, half naked with the remains of his blue and white dress hanging from his waist, kneels at the foot of the steps, where his father and other members of his family greet him. Behind is a white horse, from which a stag is being removed, while a calf is being pulled and pushed by two men for a sacrifice.

On the right in the middle distance are two more horses and a groom, beside a fountain, behind which is a castle, lake, trees and hills, while on the left is the house, with a balustraded garden.

For details and history, see No. 135.

Dutch School, XVII Century

137. VILLAGE SCHOOL

Wood, 12 × 14 in.

An old woman with a brown cap on her head and a white scarf round her neck, brown coat, white apron and blue skirt, is seated on the left at a desk in a wooden building. About twenty-five people of all ages are grouped round, some sitting on benches and some on the ground, holding papers and books.

Cleaned and repaired in 1952. In good condition.

Provenance: At Wilton before 1730, probably bought by Thomas, 8th Earl of Pembroke. Gambarini (p. 72), attributes it to 'Ostade, a woman teaching school, this was brother to one of the others' (sic).

Dutch or Flemish School, XVII Century

138. LANDSCAPE

Wood, 15¼ × 19¾ in.

Sunset over a distant plain is seen through a gorge. On the top of the steep cliff to the left are houses and trees, and ruins are on the right cliff, while figures and animals are passing through the gorge on a path.

Cleaned in 1934.

Provenance: Probably bought by Thomas, 8th Earl of Pembroke, at the beginning of the eighteenth century. It has been impossible to trace this painting from the insufficient descriptions in the early catalogues.

Dutch or Flemish School, XVII ? Century

139. SIR PHILIP SIDNEY MORTALLY WOUNDED AT THE BATTLE OF ZUTPHEN

Canvas, 80 × 69 in.

Sidney, on the left, supported by soldiers in armour, is seated on a slope, looking with a pale face at a dying soldier, surrounded by his comrades, a little below him to the right. The battle goes on in the landscape background.

This painting represents the well-known scene when Sidney, on being offered a glass of water, is supposed to have said, pointing to the wounded soldier, 'His need is greater than mine'.

Sidney was born in 1554, and died from his wounds in 1586. He spent much of his time at Wilton, where he wrote 'The Arcadia', which he dedicated to his sister Mary, third wife of Henry, 2nd Earl of Pembroke.

Cleaned in 1952. Some damages in the lower half.

Provenance: Bought by Sidney, Lord Herbert of Lea, probably between 1840 and 1861. (Lady Herbert's manuscripts notes at Wilton.)

The attribution to a painter of the Dutch or Flemish School may be incorrect; Mr John Walker, Director of the National Gallery of Art, Washington, thinks that it could be by an obscure seventeenth-century Spanish painter.

Dutch or Flemish School

140. HENRY DE VERE, 18TH EARL OF OXFORD (1593–1625)

Wood, 24×15 in.

Full length, standing, turned slightly to the left; his long brown hair and pointed beard fall over the white collar of his brown laced tunic; white stockings show below the full breeches, and he wears high black boots with spurs. To his left is a table, covered with a red cloth, on which rests his black hat, and white wand of office as Lord Great Chamberlain.

Cleaned and repaired in 1936.

Provenance: This painting was presented to the Hon. Sidney Herbert, when a boy of eleven, by a Mr G. Watson Taylor of Earlstoke Park, Wiltshire, in 1821, in the belief that it was a portrait of Philip, 4th Earl of Pembroke, by Cornelius Johnson. (Letter at Wilton from Mr Watson Taylor to Sidney Herbert, dated November 8, 1821.)

The correct identification was made in 1953 by Mr Oliver Millar, who considers the painter to be closer to Mytens than to Johnson; there is a full-scale version at Omberley Court, Worcester.

Though Mr Watson Taylor was probably unaware of it, Lord Oxford's sister, Susan, was married to the 4th Lord Pembroke.

Anglo-Dutch School, XVII Century

141. KING CHARLES I AND QUEEN HENRIETTA MARIA WITH WILLIAM, 3RD EARL OF PEMBROKE, LORD STEWARD, AND HIS BROTHER PHILIP, 1ST EARL OF MONTGOMERY, LORD CHAMBERLAIN, INSIDE WHITEHALL PALACE OR DURHAM HOUSE   *Plate* 51

Canvas, 38×46 in.

The King and Queen stand to the right just within the doorway of a paved hall, attended by Lord Pembroke and Lord Montgomery; the King wears a black hat, a grey-brown doublet trimmed with silver, brown breeches and green stockings, and black cloak, with gloves on both hands. From his neck hangs the Garter ribbon. The Queen wears a green dress, with pearl necklace and ear-rings. The brothers are in black court dress, with white lace collars, and the Garter ribbons, and carry their wands of office. Above the three steps in the centre of the picture is the Court Dwarf, Sir Jeffery Hudson, in scarlet, with three dogs. On the balustrade is a parrot. Behind is another panelled hall, with pictures on the walls. A long perspective behind the dwarf shows a gallery with a woman looking out of a window.

Old re-paints removed, and picture restored and cleaned in 1957–8.

Provenance: A. A. H. Wykeham, Esq. (formerly of Tythrop), a descendant of the Hon. James Herbert (No. 42), who married Jane Spiller, of Tythrop. Purchased by Sidney, Lord Herbert, at Christie's, June 21, 1957, lot 84, for sixty guineas.

Versions: At Kensington Palace (Oliver Millar, *Tudor, Stuart and Georgian Pictures in the Royal Collection*, London, 1963, No. 314) formerly at Windsor; Messrs William Hallsborough Ltd. (1947) ex Lord Chesham and Lord Poulett. In this version, the colours of the dresses are different, and the paintings on the walls are landscapes instead of the Titians then in the Royal collection.

Earl of Haddington (Tyninghame, Scotland): slightly larger, and some variations.

Literature: 'A Charles I Conversation Piece' by Margaret Toynbee, *The Burlington Magazine*, Vol. LXXXIX, 1947, pp. 245–7.

Mr Oliver Millar, who has done much research into the Kensington Palace and Wilton versions, dates them about 1635, the figures being based on portraits by Mytens and Van Dyck.

FLEMISH SCHOOL

Jan Frans van Bloemen

1662–1749

Born in Antwerp; visited Italy as a young man and studied under Antonius Goubau. He was influenced by Claude and Gaspar Poussin, and after settling in Rome (where he died), he painted a large number of landscapes of views near Rome. He became known as Orizonte.

142. LANDSCAPE WITH FIGURES

Canvas, $26\frac{1}{4} \times 19\frac{1}{2}$ in.

Seven or eight figures are seen in the foreground, some walking, and others sitting by a small lake, in a rocky landscape of hills and woods with castles and a village in the middle distance.

Cleaned in 1960. In fair condition.

Provenance: First recorded by Gambarini (p. 52) as by Orizonte; bought by Thomas, 8th Earl of Pembroke.

Pieter Brueghel the Younger

1564–1638

Born in Brussels, son of his more famous father; worked mainly in Antwerp, where he died.

143. 'THE BIRD TRAP'   *Plate 43*

Wood, $14\frac{1}{2} \times 22$ in.

Numerous figures are seen skating and walking on the frozen river, which runs through the snow-covered village; in the right foreground are two large trees, near which is the bird trap, from which a rope is tied to a window in a cottage.

Cleaned and repaired in 1936. In very good condition.

One of a dozen or more versions of this well known subject; two of the best examples are in (1) the Kunsthistorisches Museum in Vienna, and (2) the Leonard Koetser Gallery, London (1964) ex Lady

Price Thomas collection, dated 1601 and 1604 respectively.

Provenance: Acquired in the eighteenth century.

Jan (Velvet) Brueghel

1568–1625

The younger son of Pieter Brueghel the Elder; born in Brussels, entered in 1597 the Guild of Antwerp, where he died.

144. WINTER SCENE IN A VILLAGE   *Plate 44*

Wood, $17\frac{1}{2} \times 28\frac{1}{2}$ in.

Numerous figures are walking and skating on a frozen stream, which runs through the middle of the snow-covered village; farm carts and horses are in the right foreground, and in the background near the houses and shops, outside which people are gathered.

Blisters laid, cleaned and repaired in 1932. In fair condition.

Provenance: At Wilton before 1730; probably bought by Thomas, 8th Earl of Pembroke. Gambarini (p. 67) says that there were a pair, one Winter, the other Summer, by Velvet Bruegel, which may be No. 145.

? Pieter Bruegel the Elder

c. 1530–1569

or Jan (Velvet) Brueghel

1568–1625

145. A VILLAGE FAIR

Wood, $15\frac{1}{4} \times 22\frac{1}{2}$ in.

A multitude of small, gaily dressed figures are seen in groups, some dancing, while others are on horses or in boats or in a carriage on the edge of a village with hills behind; on the right is a castle surrounded by a moat, over which is a bridge, and on the water are four boats.

Cleaned in 1952. Cleaning revealed that, at some time, two thirds of the painting had been cut out of or let into the whole of the panel which on the back is unaltered. It is difficult to account for this alteration as the one third seems to be part of the original composition.

Provenance: At Wilton before 1730; Gambarini (page 67) records: 'Jan Brugel (Velvet), a pair, one Winter, the other Summer, a Fair.' Probably bought by Thomas, 8th Earl of Pembroke.

Faintly stamped on the back are what appear to be two open hands above a castle or coat of arms, to the left of which is some kind of flower or rosette. These marks may give a clue as to the origin of the painting.

School of Hans Eworth
? 1520–? 1574

Eworth entered the Painter's Guild at Antwerp in 1540; about 1545 he came to England, where he worked until his death.

146. SIR WILLIAM HERBERT, 1ST EARL OF PEM-
BROKE, K.G. (1507–1570)   *Plate* 1
Wood, 79×44 in.

Full length, standing, wearing a black and gold doublet and trunk hose, black cloak studded with gold buttons, black stockings and shoes, flat black and gold hat. Long grey moustache and beard, which falls over a white ruff. The jewelled George of the Garter is suspended on a long gold chain from his neck. His left arm holds a pair of gloves in front of his sword, and his right arm holds the top of a white staff. The Garter is below his left knee. A small brown dog is seated at his feet, next to a high-backed Tudor chair. The background is an olive-green curtain, on which is the following inscription: 'William Harbert Earle of Penbrooke, Lord Steward of Howshold to Quene Elizabethae sy for bountifull and good manners highly estemed in his tyme. He died the . . . year of his age in . . .' Over part of this inscription is painted the white Lumley label or cartellino which says 'William Herbert, created Earle of Pembroke 1551'. On the base of the pillar on the left is painted 'Aetatis 66. A.D. 1567'.

This inscription is somewhat later than the painting, and should read 60 instead of 66.

Cleaned, re-paints removed, blisters secured, repaired in 1934 and in 1963. In good condition, retaining nearly all the original paint.

William, the founder of the family, was the son of Sir Richard Herbert of Ewyas, Glamorgan; in 1527 at the age of 20, according to Aubrey, he fought and killed a man in Bristol, escaped to Wales, and from there to France, where he joined the army, distinguishing himself so greatly that Francis I recommended him to Henry VIII. Returning to England, he married c. 1534, Anne, daughter of Sir Thomas Parr of Kendal and sister to Catherine, who became the King's sixth and last wife in 1543. But even before he became related by marriage to Henry VIII, William Herbert was in high favour; in 1542 he was granted a coat of arms, and crest, and two years later he was given the Abbey and lands of Wilton by the King. He was now a great power in England, and was made an executor of Henry VIII's will and appointed one of the Guardians to Edward VI. In 1549 he was installed as a Knight of the Garter and made Master of the Horse. In October 1551, Edward VI created him Lord Herbert of Cardiff and Earl of Pembroke. He was made a Privy Councillor and President of the Council in Wales, where he still retained his immense estates in Monmouth and Glamorgan. He had the Abbey at Wilton pulled down, and built himself a house, where he entertained Edward VI in 1552. He retained the favour of Queen Mary on her accession, welcomed Philip of Spain at Southampton, and was present at their marriage in 1554 at Winchester. In 1557 he was appointed Captain-General of the English Army sent to defend Calais, and won the battle of St Quentin, taking prisoner the Constable of France, Annas de Montmorency, and the Duke of Montpensier.

Queen Elizabeth I retained his services, and he continued to wield much power until his death at Hampton Court on March 17, 1570. He was buried in Old St Paul's Cathedral.

Provenance: As all the Tudor portraits of the 1st and 2nd Earls and their wives were presumably burnt in the fire of 1647, this portrait was probably bought by the 4th or 5th Earl about 1650 from the collection of John Lord Lumley, who had painted labels added to many of the portraits which belonged to him about 1590–1600. The picture is listed in the Lumley

Inventory of 1590, which is owned by the Earl of Scarbrough. Aubrey saw it at Wilton about 1655, and in his description he says: 'This William . . . had a little cur dog which loved him and the Earl loved the dog; when the Earle dyed, the dog would not goe from his master's body, but pined away, and dyed under the hearse: the picture of which dog is under (sic) his picture in the gallery at Wilton.' The dog was undoubtedly added by another hand, and is badly drawn and painted.

Exhibited: Tudor Exhibition, 1890.

References: Aubrey's Brief Lives; James Kennedy's Catalogue (1751) and subsequent eighteenth century catalogues; Passavant; Waagen.

Portraits: At Holyrood Palace, three-quarter length, in armour, signed 'Aersten, 1557', formerly called Henry, 2nd Earl; full length in black costume, property of the Duke of Leeds, on loan to the Ministry of Works; at Knole; full length with others in large picture of Edward VI presenting the Charter to Bridewell Hospital.

Version: No. 147 below.

School of Hans Eworth

147. SIR WILLIAM HERBERT, 1ST EARL OF PEMBROKE, K.G. (1507–1570)

Wood, 35½ × 27¼ in.

Three-quarter length, standing, nearly full face, wearing a pink dress slashed with white and embroidered with silver, over which is a black coat embroidered with silver and slashed to show a white fur lining. A black cap is on his head, and a white ruff round his neck. Over the dress is the chain and jewel of the Order of the Garter. In his right hand is a wand, and in his left a pair of gloves. Right background is part of a green curtain.

Cleaned, old re-paints removed and repaired in 1965–6.

For details of the 1st Earl, see No. 146.

Provenance: Northwick Collection. 1864 Catalogue, No. 217. E. G. Spencer-Churchill Collection, Catalogue (Borenius), No. 278 as portrait of Henry Carey, 1st Lord Hunsdon. Purchased at Christie's, June 25, 1965, for 550 guineas by Sidney, 16th Earl of Pembroke.

Frans Francken the Younger
1581–1642

Born in Antwerp, the younger son of another artist of that name, who taught him; he worked in Venice for some years before returning to Antwerp, where he died.

148. INTERIOR OF A PICTURE GALLERY
Plates 49, 52

Wood, 36¾ × 48½ in.

Four men in the left foreground stand round a table in a large room lit by two windows, examining busts and pictures on it; the rear wall is hung with pictures, and more are on the floor, on which is a small monkey and also a parrot on a perch. On a shield above the pictures is written 'Nihil est ab omni parte beatum ne jupiter quidem omnibus placet'. The right of the gallery opens onto a grand staircase and hall, in which three men are standing.

Cleaned in 1950. In very good condition.

Provenance: One of seven pictures left by General Philip Goldsworthy to George, 11th Earl of Pembroke, at the beginning of the nineteenth century as a 'Gallery in Florence'.

Wrongly stated by Wilkinson to have been in the collection before 1730 and painted by J. B. Francken.

Literature: S. Speth-Holterhoff, *Les Peintres Flamands de Cabinets d'Amateurs au XVII siecle.* (Brussels, 1957), pp. 80–81, Pl. 20.

Hugo van der Goes
? 1435–1482

Born at Ghent; little is known about his early life. He worked in Bruges and Louvain. His paintings are rare, the most famous being the Portinari Altarpiece in the Uffizi Gallery.

149. THE ADORATION OF THE SHEPHERDS
Plate 32

Wood, 13 × 14 in.

The Virgin, in the centre, wearing a deep-blue dress and cloak, with her hands crossed on her breast, looks down on the infant Christ lying on a white drapery in a straw-filled square manger. To the right is St Joseph, wearing a crimson robe, his hands in prayer, kneeling at the foot of the manger; the heads of two angels appear between him and the Virgin. Behind him an ox and an ass are seen, and beyond them through an opening can be seen small figures of shepherds and sheep on a hill, over which appears an angel in the sky. To the left, in violet and grey, are two angels kneeling, gazing at the head of Christ; behind them, leaning forward are two more shepherds, one in green and one in black.

In the earlier catalogues this masterpiece was attributed to Van Eyck; a false signature to this effect had been added in the sixteenth or seventeenth century, and cannot be removed without damaging the original paint. In the nineteenth century the panel was neglected; it split vertically in three pieces and was found in this condition in a drawer at Wilton in 1900. The panels were joined by Buttery, who also cleaned the painting, which retains virtually all the original paint. It was revarnished in 1932, and in 1955 some blisters were secured.

Provenance: Perhaps bought by Philip, 4th Earl, before 1650, or Thomas, 8th Earl, before 1730.

Exhibited: Masterpieces through four centuries. Knoedler, London, 1935; *Dutch and Flemish Painting.* Slatter Gallery, London, 1949.

Literature: M. J. Friedländer, *Die altniederländische Malerei,* vol. IV, p. 127, No. 16.

Jan Gossaert (Mabuse)
? 1472–1533

Born at Maubeuge in Hainault; Master of the Guild of St Luke in Antwerp in 1503. He travelled widely in Italy before returning to the Netherlands, where he died.

150. THE CHILDREN OF CHRISTIAN II, KING OF DENMARK   *Plate 34*

Wood, 12¾×15¾ in.

The children are seen seated, full face, at a green table, on which are two apples and three cherries. The eldest son, John, is in the centre, dressed in black, wearing a large flat black hat; to the right is his sister Christina (afterwards Duchess of Milan), in black with ermine sleeves, and on her head a black and white hood; to the left is the younger sister,

Dorothea, wearing black, with ermine sleeves, with a square-cut white top to her dress.

Cleaned and repaired in 1934. In good condition.

Provenance: Formerly called the children of Henry VII in the eighteenth century catalogues; this painting may have been in the sixteenth or seventeenth century collection, or it may have been bought by Thomas, 8th Earl of Pembroke. It is included in the 1731 Gambarini catalogue.

It does not compare very favourably with the original version in the Royal Collection, or that at Longford Castle (Earl of Radnor), and appears to be unfinished, as the ornaments round the necks of the children and on their dresses are absent, as are the stalks and leaves on the cherries in the foreground.

Exhibited: Manchester, *The Art Treasures of the United Kingdom,* 1857; New Gallery, London, 1901–2.

Versions: Royal Collection, Hampton Court; Earl of Radnor (Longford Castle); formerly at Corsham Court (Lord Methuen).

Literature: M. J. Friedländer, *Die altniederländische Malerei,* vol. VIII, p. 164, No. 79A.

Alexander Keirincx
1600–1652

When only nineteen, he became a master in the Guild of St. Luke. Visited England and Scotland in the reign of Charles I.

151. CEPHALUS AND PROCRIS   *Plate 61*

Wood, 19½×25 in.

Cephalus stands on a grass track in a wood with a dog beside him, staring distractedly at Procris, who lies at the foot of a tree with an arrow through her heart; two figures are seen running through the wood in the background. On the right is a lake on which are two swans. The story is told by Ovid, *Metamorphoses,* Book VII.

Cleaned in 1933, and blisters secured in 1955. In good condition.

Provenance: At Wilton before 1730; under different attributions in eighteenth and nineteenth centuries. At Pembroke House, Whitehall, in 1827.

Version: Alte Pinakothek, Munich (No. 2059).

Frans Luycx or van Leux
? 1604–1660?

Born in Antwerp, studied under Rubens; Court painter of Emperor Ferdinand III of Austria.

152. A NOBLEMAN HAWKING

Canvas, 86×83 in.

The man stands, lifesize, on the left, against a background of trees, wearing a black hat with a white plume, a long black fur-lined coat, with a yellow waistcoat over a white shirt, long brown breeches, white stockings with lace over the knees, and long black boots. His right hand is in the pocket of his coat, while his left is raised holding a small piece of meat before the hawk, which is sitting on the gloved right wrist of a smiling boy dressed in a blue and black coat with white breeches and black boots, holding a feathered hat in his left hand. A brown greyhound type of dog, with the face of another just seen, is sitting behind the boy, and on the right behind the boy a brown horse is grazing. A gun is attached to the saddle.

Relined, cleaned in 1920. Much rubbed and considerably damaged.

Provenance: Not identified in any of the eighteenth century catalogues, though Wilkinson says, without quoting an authority, that it was left to Henry, 9th Earl of Pembroke. It is possible that it came to him through his maternal grandfather, Sir Mathew Decker, who was Dutch by birth, settled in England at the beginning of the eighteenth century and was knighted by George I.

School of Bernard van Orley
c. 1490–1541

Van Orley was greatly influenced by the work of Raphael; in 1515 he settled in Brussels, where he became famous, painting altar-pieces, religious subjects and some portraits.

153. THE VIRGIN AND CHILD, WITH ST ANNE AND AN ANGEL   *Plate* 35

Wood, 35×22¼ in.

The Virgin, seated, wears a dark-green robe with a red skirt, and holds the infant Christ, who is half standing, on her lap. Behind stands St Anne, her arms outstretched, with a white hood on her head and round her neck, wearing a black, grey and brown dress. To the left the Angel, wearing a yellow dress with pink sleeves, bends over the cradle, on which his right hand rests, and with his outstretched left arm, touches the Child's back. In the background are columns and a window, through which is seen a landscape. The painting has an arched top.

Cleaned and repaired in 1934. In very good condition.

Provenance: At Wilton before 1730. Probably bought by Thomas, 8th Earl of Pembroke. Gambarini (p. 88) attributed it to Perugino.

Versions: Cassel Gallery, Germany (No. 25), attributed to a follower of Bernard van Orley.

Mr Keith Osborne, Walton-on-Thames (1965), attributed to Pieter Coecke van Aelst (according to information from Christie's).

Sir Peter Paul Rubens
1577–1640

Born at Siegen in Westphalia, son of a lawyer; studied under Adam van Noort; travelled and worked in Italy, Spain, France and England, where he was knighted by Charles I in 1630. He had settled in Antwerp in 1608, and died there in 1640.

154. CHRIST, ST JOHN AND TWO ANGELS
Plate 46

Wood, 37½×48 in.

Christ is seated on the right facing towards St John, whose back is turned with his left arm round a lamb's neck; one of the angels on the left is half holding up the lamb, while the other in the right background, half hidden by the Infant Christ, holds a bunch of grapes. In the right foreground are fruit and vegetables and behind them is a tree.

As in a number of paintings by Rubens, Frans Snyders (1579–1657) painted the fruit and vegetables in this version as well in the others enumerated below.

Painted about 1620.

Cleaned, re-paints removed and repaired in 1935. In good condition, but the panel is slightly warped.

Provenance: At Wilton before 1730; Gambarini says that 'this picture was brought from Spain by Monsieur Grammont when he was Ambassador there, the King of Spain persuaded Rubens to part with it who always intended to keep it'.

Versions: Berlin-Dahlem, Staatliche Museen, No. 779; Kunsthistorisches Museum, Vienna, No. 315; Kingston Lacy, Dorset (Ralph Bankes, Esq.) – slightly larger and the children play with birds; Schleissheim Gallery; Private collection, Antwerp. In the Vienna version, the background and fruit are different.

Cowdry records that Hoare of Bath made a very fine copy in crayons.

Engraved in mezzotint by John Dean.

155. LANDSCAPE WITH A SHEPHERD   *Plate 45*

Canvas, 27 × 32 in.

Centre a stream flowing left; in the left foreground is a clump of trees, and in the foreground a foot-bridge with a shepherd in a red jacket leaning on a crook. At his feet are four sheep, and further on fifteen others; trees in the right background and centre middle distance, with the sun setting on the extreme left, where there are a pair of swans. A huntsman and dogs are seen in the centre of a distant gap in the wood.

Cleaned in 1935 and 1958. In very good condition.

Provenance: In James Kennedy's catalogue, 1758, probably bought by Henry, 9th Earl of Pembroke.

Versions: National Gallery (No. 2924, on wood); before 1913 in the collection of the Earl of Carlisle. ?Freiherr von Speck zu Sternberg, Lützschena, Germany.

Literature: Horace Walpole, *Anecdotes of Painting*, Vol. I, p. 310; J. Smith, *Catalogue Raisonné*, No. 859.

After Rubens

156. THE ASSUMPTION OF THE VIRGIN *Plate* 48

Wood, 13½ × 9½ in.

The Virgin in a pink and blue robe with light brown drapery over her head and arms stands rising on a cloud, below which are eight cherubs, one holding a bunch of flowers. In the two top corners and below her extended left arm are the heads in twos and threes of more cherubs.

Cleaned in 1934. In good condition.

Provenance: Gambarini says it was in the Arundel collection as by Rubens. It is in fact a seventeenth-century copy of the upper half, with minor variations, of the engraving by Schelte a Bolswert, about 1650, illustrated by Rooses, *L'Oeuvre de P. P. Rubens*, II, pl. 122 (Antwerp, 1888), in which he reverses the design of the oil sketch by Rubens which the Prince Regent bought in 1816 (Royal Collection, Buckingham Palace, Cat. p. 87, No. 108).

Bought by Thomas, 8th Earl of Pembroke.

Copy after Rubens
Late XVII or early XVIII Century

157. THE ADORATION OF THE SHEPHERDS

Copper on wood, 8¾ × 12 in.

The Virgin, in red and blue, is seated behind the head of the manger, on which lies the Child, draped in white; an old woman with a white cap on her head, wearing a white jacket and blue skirt, kneels beside the manger, while grouped behind her are three shepherds and a tall young woman in blue, grey and mauve, carrying a large brass pitcher on her head. On the left is part of a donkey, and the head of a cow, behind which is St Joseph, in yellow. Above him are the heads of three cherubs.

Cleaned and repaired in 1952. In fair condition.

This is a copy of the painting by Rubens on panel in the Museum in Marseilles, which is part of the predella to the triptych for St-Jean, Malines, which was taken to Paris in 1796, only part of it being returned to the church in 1815. It was engraved by Lucas Vorsterman.

Provenance: At Wilton before 1730; probably bought by Thomas, 8th Earl of Pembroke.

Sir Anthony van Dyck
1599–1641

Born at Antwerp, son of a silk merchant; studied under Rubens for five years. Travelled widely in Italy from 1621 to 1626 before returning to Antwerp, and then went to England, where Charles I appointed him Court Painter and knighted him in 1632. He worked also in Brussels and Antwerp, before returning to London, where he died.

158. PHILIP, 4TH EARL OF PEMBROKE, AND HIS FAMILY   *Plates* II, 4, 6

Canvas, 11 ft. by 17 ft.

Lord Pembroke, seated in the centre of the picture, wears a black court dress, white lace collar and cuffs, blue stockings and black shoes with large bows; the Garter Star is embroidered on his left sleeve, the Collar and Greater George of the Garter is worn from the shoulders, and the Garter itself is below his left knee. In his left hand he holds his wand of office as Lord Chamberlain, and he points with his right hand to his daughter-in-law, Lady Mary Villiers, who is dressed in white satin with black bows and stands sideways below him on a step, with her head turned to the right. On his left, seated beside him, is his second wife, Anne Clifford, daughter of the Earl of Cumberland, and widow of the Duke of Dorset, dressed in black, with her hands folded across her lap. On her left stands Lord Pembroke's only daughter, Sophia, wearing a low-cut blue dress, pearl necklace, ear-rings, and pearls in her hair, turned inwards towards the left, her right hand across her waist, her left hand in the right hand of her husband, Robert Dormer, 2nd Baron Dormer, and 1st Earl of Carnarvon, who stands sideways, a step below her, his head turned to the left, wearing a brown satin 'Cavalier' suit with high boots, his left hand on his waist above his sword. To the left of Mary Villiers and slightly behind her, two steps higher, stands Charles, Lord Herbert, sideways, looking across his father to his sister and brother-in-law. He wears a rich red satin court dress, with white slashed sleeves, white lace collar, red stockings and shoes with large bows; his right arm is on his waist, and his left arm is raised holding up a cape. Behind him, standing, nearly full face, is his brother Philip, with long red hair, wearing a yellow satin court dress, with white lace collar and cuffs, yellow stockings and boots; his right hand is across his chest, and his left hand is hidden. Below him on the left of the picture, wearing brown and black suits, grouped with dogs, and holding books, in a variety of attitudes and gazing upwards, are three younger sons, James, William and John. In the top left hand corner three more children, who died as infants, are seen floating in on clouds as angels. Below them is the sky and a tree, and between two large columns is a curtain or tapestry with the coat of arms of the family, and on the right a green curtain, and draped over the steps is a carpet.

Cleaned, old re-paints removed and repaired in 1915; surface cleaned again in 1932 and 1951.

The following manuscript is preserved at Wilton:

'Account of what has been done to the Family Picture, (and what will be necessary in future), in 1773 and 1774.

'The old oil varnish was taken off; it was new lined with a strong Russia ticking, painted with two bodies of colour to prevent the damp from occasioning any blisters, by softening the paste which holds the Canvas's together, as also to prevent any attempt in future to line it again, the colours being so very rotten in many parts that by any attempt of that nature it is probable they would fall to pieces. In some degree to remedy that defect after the dirt and the old varnish were taken off, it was nourished by rubbing it with fine white poppy oil so long as it appeared to receive it; then the putty and bad wax with which the cracks had been filled, were taken out and supplied by a preparation of the finest white wax as usual on such occasions, and where it was necessary in the background and some other places of no material consequence, repainted; the glazings or transparent colours which had evaporated by the length of time the picture has been painted, were slightly restored with fresh, particularly in the blue, the pink, the yellow drapery and the trees. After that was compleated, it was varnished twice with Wall's finest Copal varnish, the quality of which is so very hard that dirt can only affect the exterior surface and not the picture. In future it is supposed (accident excepted) that the picture will not require anything more to be done to it. Perhaps it may be necessary in six eight or ten years to give it a new coat of varnish, and to always repeat it at the expiration of that period, upon which occasion an Apple or an Onion cut in half to rub it with all over will be sufficient to remove the dirt; then it must be washed with a sponge and soft water, milk warm, after which the varnish may be put on in one or two coats as is thought necessary. Particular care must be taken that it is not a spirit varnish, but Wall's oil Copal varnish.

'N. B. Wall, Japaner, lives at No: 25 Long Acre.'

When this severe treatment was applied to the picture, it was but 140 years old. It is an interesting but alarming account of what picture restorers did in the eighteenth century. As the statement truly says, Wall's Copal varnish is very hard and thick, and it has been extremely difficult to remove even with modern methods; and quite apart from the size of the picture which is composed of three canvases stitched together horizontally, the fact that it was relined in the fashion described above, has given it a very uneven surface. It is framed in such a way as part of the wall decoration that it is virtually impossible to take it down and examine the back, even if such an immense canvas could be laid on the ground. So the eighteenth-century re-lining instructions appear to be irrevocable.

Provenance: Commissioned by Philip, 4th Earl of Pembroke, and painted in London, 1634–5, where it hung in Durham House off the Strand, a house leased by the family because Baynards Castle, bought by the first Earl, situated on the Thames near the Tower of London, was considered too old, damp and inconvenient in every way. The painting remained at Durham House until it was moved to Wilton about 1652, when the house, reconstructed by Inigo Jones and John Webb following the fire of 1647, contained the new State rooms, the great 'Double Cube' room having been designed to take this family group and nine of the other paintings by Van Dyck.

Versions: A much reduced and greatly altered version, attributed to Lely, is in the Hermitage Gallery, Leningrad. A drawing for this is in the possession of Mr Cottrel-Dormer at Rousham.
Gainsborough Dupont painted a small copy, now in the possession of the Dowager Viscountess Hambleden.
Another much reduced version is at Castle Ashby (Marquess of Northampton).
At Holkham Hall (Earl of Leicester) is a small drawing which is thought to be Van Dyck's sketch for the painting, and another similar one, done from the painting, belongs to the Hon. David Herbert, which may be the one formerly at Highclere.
In the British Museum are sketches by Van Dyck for Robert Dormer, Earl of Carnarvon, and his wife Sophia Herbert in black chalk heightened with white on light brown paper ($19\frac{3}{8} \times 11\frac{1}{2}$ in.); Lady Mary Villiers ($18\frac{1}{4} \times 11\frac{3}{4}$ in.); and Philip Herbert, later 5th Earl ($13\frac{1}{2} \times 8\frac{7}{8}$ in.).
In the Accademia Carrara di Belle Arti, Bergamo, is a small copy (34×45 in.) of the late seventeenth or early eighteenth century.

Literature: References are too numerous to mention. It is first recorded in the Egerton MS. 1636, in the British Museum, 'The Earle of Pembrookes Collections of Paintings at Durham Howse: a mighty large piece of the Ea: of Pembrooke & all his family by Vandyke'. Aubrey, Evelyn, Vertue, Gambarini and his successors, as well as nineteenth and twentieth century art historians and others give descriptions in their catalogues, diaries and notes.

Engraved: Bernard Baron.

159. WILLIAM, 3RD EARL OF PEMBROKE, K.G. (1580–1630) *Plate 2*

Canvas, 87×54 in.

Full length, turned slightly to the left, he stands in front of a column and crimson curtain, wearing a black court dress with a wide white lace ruff and cuffs; over the dress is a black cloak, on the left sleeve of which is the Garter Star, the arm resting against the column, and the hand holds his wand of office as Lord Steward to Charles I; the right arm is extended downwards. Black hair, moustache and beard. Below the ruff is the blue riband and George of the Garter, and round his waist is a gold embroidered sword belt.

Cleaned, re-paints removed in 1925, and surface cleaned again in 1936 and 1962. Like most of the Van Dycks, this portrait had been badly rubbed and restored in previous centuries, and the surface is somewhat uneven, but the face and top part of the picture is in fairly good condition.

William, Lord Pembroke, was born at Wilton in 1580, the eldest son by his third wife, Mary Sidney, of Henry, 2nd Earl; his godmother was Queen Elizabeth I, and his godfathers the Earls of Warwick and Leicester. He went to New College, Oxford, aged thirteen, and at the age of twenty-one succeeded his father. In 1603, he was made a Knight of the Garter, in 1607 Governor of Portsmouth, and in 1615, Lord Chamberlain to James I. In 1626 he became Chancellor of the University of Oxford, and Lord Steward to Charles I. He had married in 1604 Mary Talbot, daughter of the 7th Earl of Shrewsbury, and had two sons in 1616 and 1621, both of whom died in infancy. He was a scholar and poet, and a friend of the great literary figures of the early years of the seventeenth century, and it was to him and his younger brother Philip, who succeeded him, that the First Folios of Shakespeare were dedicated as 'The most noble and incomparable pair of brethren'. He died in 1630.

Provenance: If Gambarini and tradition are to be believed, this portrait was painted from the life-size bronze statue in the Bodleian Library at Oxford (given by Thomas, 8th Earl) though it is not at all similar; that it is a posthumous portrait there is little doubt, as he died in April 1630, two years before Van Dyck came to England.

Portraits of the 3rd Earl are at Windsor Castle (Oliver Millar, *Tudor, Stuart and Early Georgian*

Pictures in the Royal Collection, 1963, No. 107), by Van Somer; at Kensington Palace (*ib.*, No. 314), Anglo-Dutch School; in U.S.A. property of Mr Herbert Boone, ex collection of Lord Ailwyn of Honingham, Norfolk, 1936, purchased by Leggatt Bros; by D. Mytens; at Breamore, Hants, property of Sir Westrow Hulse, Bt., by or after D. Mytens; at Wilton, by D. Mytens (No. 119), and School of Mytens (No. 120); the property of the Earl of Clarendon, by or after Van Dyck, on loan to the Plymouth Art Gallery; the Earl of Powis, Powis Castle, Welshpool, three-quarter length, attributed to Abraham Blyenberch, dated 1617, oil on panel, 44×31½ in.

Engraving: Simon Passens, 1617 (after the half length by Paul van Somer at Windsor Castle).
R. Cooper (after the three-quarter length by Cornelius Jonson).
H. T. Ryall, and W. Holl (after the full length by Van Dyck at Wilton).

160. PHILIP, 4TH EARL OF PEMBROKE AND 1ST EARL OF MONTGOMERY, K.G. (1584–1649)

Canvas, 87×54 in.

Full length, standing, with his right foot on a shallow step, half turned to the left looking over his left shoulder; his long hair falling over the deep white lace collar of his black court dress, which he wears with knee breeches, grey-blue stockings with large pink and white striped bows below the knees, and large bows on his black shoes. With his right hand he holds up a large black cloak, on which is embroidered the Star of the Order of the Garter, with the blue Riband of the Order hanging from his neck. In his left hand he holds the wand of office as Lord Chamberlain. Background of a red curtain and column.

Cleaned in 1925; so uneven was the surface, that it was found necessary in 1936 to re-line it, when it was discovered that on some previous re-lining, probably in the eighteenth century, the lining canvas had been put on with a thin layer of cement which was showing through. This had to be chipped away, and it was then re-lined, and old repaints removed. But the paint had, in the past, been rubbed and apparently scrubbed to remove old varnish, and is now very thin. Most of the picture, including the face and hands, retain very little of Van Dyck's brush work. It had to be varnished again in 1962–3.

Philip was the second son of the 2nd Earl and Mary Sidney; at an early age he was brought to the Court at London, and in 1603 was made a Knight of the Bath. James I created him Baron Herbert of Shurland, and Earl of Montgomery in 1605, when he was twenty-one years old; three years later he made him a Knight of the Garter, and a Gentleman of the Bedchamber. He married in 1604 Lady Susan Vere, daughter of the 17th Earl of Oxford, in Whitehall Palace; James I gave her away, and Anne of Denmark was also present.

With his elder brother William, he was a patron of the arts and letters, and they held the offices of Lord Steward and Lord Chamberlain to James I and Charles I. In 1628 his wife died, having had nine children, three of whom died as infants (see No. 158). In 1630 he married Anne Clifford, daughter of the 3rd Earl of Cumberland and widow of Richard Sackville, Earl of Dorset, but they had no children.

In the same year he succeeded his brother as 4th Earl of Pembroke, and Chancellor of Oxford University, of which office he was deprived in the Civil War owing to his desertion of the King.

Apart from the commissions executed by Van Dyck for him, he collected pictures on a large scale, and exchanged a number of them as well as drawings with Charles I, but few remain at Wilton today. He was probably painted more often than anybody except the King by a number of different artists, and the list of portraits below, which may not be complete, gives their present location.

Version: Identical with the Wilton portrait, by Van Dyck, the property of the Earl of Clarendon, on loan to the Ministry of Works, House of Lords.

Portraits: Standing, full length, in Garter robes, probably the earliest portrait of him, about 1610–15, by the 'Curtain Master' (Audley End.)
Three-quarter length, seated, in black dress with white lace wearing the Garter, by Van Somer or Mytens. (Marquis of Salisbury, Hatfield House.)
A replica of the Hatfield portrait. (Duke of Portland, Welbeck.)
Three-quarter length, wearing a brown dress, with Garter riband, and carrying a wand of office. (Marquis of Bath, Longleat.)
Similar to the Longleat portrait. (Marquis of Exeter, Burghley House, and in the National Gallery of Victoria, Melbourne, Australia, ex collection Mr Baldwin-Childe, Kyre Park, Tenbury.)
Head and shoulders. (National Portrait Gallery, London, No. 1489.)
Full length, wearing robes and Garter Insignia, with

a coronet on the table. (Council House, Bristol, of which he was elected High Steward in 1635.)

Half length, full face, standing, by Cornelius Johnson. (Lord Egremont, Petworth.)

Full length, wearing black dress with white lace collar, and white slashed sleeves. (Earl of Warwick, Warwick Castle.)

Three-quarter length, in brown dress, white lace collar, slashed sleeves, wearing Garter riband. (Mr Herbert Boone, U.S.A., ex Tythrop sale, Agnews, 1934.)

Copy of figure in family group at Wilton. (Earl of Carnarvon, Highclere Castle.)

Three-quarter length, wearing a brown doublet with slashed sleeves and white lace collar; the wand of office is in his right hand and he wears a sword. From his neck is suspended the riband of the Garter and lesser 'George'. (Earl of Stamford, Dunham Massey Hall.)

Three-quarter length, standing, wearing brown dress, sleeves slashed with white, lace collar, and Garter riband from the neck and Star on the left sleeve, the gloved left hand holding the wand of office, School of Mytens. (Appleby Castle, Westmorland. 1954.)

In the conversation piece with his brother, and Charles I and Henrietta Maria. (Windsor Castle, Oliver Millar, *The Tudor, Stuart and Early Georgian Pictures in the Royal Collection*, 1963, No. 314.)

The same at Wilton (No. 141) and at Tyninghame. (Lord Haddington).

Full length, standing, by Mytens at Wilton (No. 118).

Head and shoulders, artist unknown, at Wilton (No. 94).

Full length, standing, by Hendrik Pot, at Wilton (No. 123).

Engraving: Robertus van Voerst (after the full length by Van Dyck at Wilton).

Robertus van Voerst (after the head and shoulders by Mytens).

Simon Passens.

E. Scriven (after the seated portrait by Van Dyck in the family group at Wilton).

W. Holl (after the seated portrait by Van Dyck in the family group at Wilton).

161. PHILIP, 5TH EARL OF PEMBROKE (1621–1669)

Canvas, 50 × 40 in.

Three-quarter length, standing, full face, his long red hair falls over a white cravat; he wears a red satin coat, the sleeves slashed with white, white cuffs, and red breeches. Over his tunic is a cuirass, over which is a red sash, which he holds with his right hand. His gloved left hand is on his right hip, against the hilt of his sword. Plain brown background.

Cleaned, repaints removed, and repaired in 1937. In good condition.

Philip was the fourth surviving son of the 4th Lord Pembroke, and married in 1639 Penelope, second daughter of Sir Robert Naunton, and nineteen-year-old widow of Paul, 2nd Viscount Bayning. They had one child William (see No. 43). She died in 1647, and in 1649 he married Catherine, daughter of Sir William Villiers, Bt., by whom he had two sons, Philip and Thomas, and five daughters. He died in 1669, having succeeded his father twenty years earlier. He led an undistinguished life, mainly at Wilton, and at Court after the Restoration, but took no part in the Civil War, though his sympathies were with the King.

Provenance: Commissioned by his father, and painted between 1635 and 1639.

Exhibited: Manchester, *The Art Treasures of the United Kingdom*, 1857; Royal Academy, 1900; Bristol, 1937.

Versions: Newburgh Priory, Yorkshire (Mrs Wombwell); originally in the collection of Lord Bellasis in the seventeenth century.

Engraving: P. Lombart (after the three-quarter length by Van Dyck at Wilton).

162. PENELOPE, LADY HERBERT (1620–1647)

Canvas, 87 × 54 in.

Full length, standing, turned slightly to the left, wearing a low-cut white satin dress, the bodice ornamented with pearls. A chain of linked pearls and sapphires goes round her waist, and low over her shoulders. Her right hand rests on a table covered by a black and brown cloth, and her left hand holds her dress. A massive column is behind the table.

Cleaned, old re-paints removed and repaired in 1933, when it was seen to have been considerably damaged, a rent two feet long being visible at the bottom of the dress. Much of the canvas had been rubbed and overpainted.

Penelope, daughter of Sir Robert Naunton, Bt., of Suffolk, was born in 1620, and married firstly, about 1635, Paul, second Viscount Bayning, who died in 1638, and secondly, Philip, Lord Herbert, afterwards 5th Earl of Pembroke, in 1639. They had one son William, later 6th Earl. She died in 1647, two years before her husband succeeded his father.

Provenance: Commissioned on her marriage in 1639, by her father-in-law.

Engraving: P. Lombart.

163. MARY VILLIERS, DUCHESS OF RICHMOND AND LENNOX (1622–1685), AND MRS GIBSON, THE DWARF (1621–1709)   Plate 56

Canvas, 87 × 51 in.

Full length, standing, the whole figure turned slightly to the left, her right foot on a shallow step, wearing a greeny-blue satin dress, over part of which, beginning at the shoulders, and falling away behind, is a brown mantle, attached to the dress with pearl clasps. Her left arm is by her side, holding the dress, and her right arm is extended taking her gloves off a tray being held up to her by Mrs Gibson, who is looking towards her; she wears a brown dress with sleeves slashed with white. Mary Villiers's ornaments are pearl ear-rings and necklace. Background of column behind Mrs Gibson, otherwise a plain brown.

Cleaned and old re-paints removed in 1932.

In common with most of the Van Dycks, it has been badly rubbed, and in places the paint is very thin, but retains more of its original paint than some of the others.

Mary Villiers was the eldest child of George, 1st Duke of Buckingham, and Catherine, daughter of the Duke of Rutland. After her father's assassination in 1628, she was 'adopted' by Charles I and brought up at Court. Though only thirteen, she was betrothed to Charles, Lord Herbert, eldest son of Philip, 4th Earl of Pembroke, in 1635, and the marriage ceremony took place in the Royal Closet at Whitehall. Within a few months, the bridegroom, who was sixteen, died of smallpox in Florence, where he had gone to join the army of the Grand Duke of Tuscany. In 1637 she married James Stuart, Duke of Richmond (see No. 172), in Lambeth Palace Chapel and was given away by the King. They had one son and one daughter. The Duke died in 1655, and she then married Colonel Thomas Howard, a brother of the Earl of Carlisle.

Anne Shepherd, wife of Richard Gibson, who was a

painter and page at the Court, had nine children, all of normal height, though her husband was also a dwarf.

Provenance: Probably painted shortly after her second marriage, and either commissioned by Philip, 4th Earl of Pembroke, her father-in-law for a few months, or bought by him.

Versions: Formerly at Newnham Paddox (Earl of Denbigh) a very good studio copy, identical with the Wilton portrait; Mary Villiers' aunt had married the Earl of Denbigh. This portrait was sold at Christie's in 1938 for £1750, and went to the Hearst collection in America, and is now, with other pictures from that collection, in the Los Angeles County Museum.

At Blenheim (Duke of Marlborough), where there is a slight variation in the background; in the Ashburnham collection, sold at Sotheby's in 1953, similar to the Blenheim portrait, but a copy.

Portraits: At Windsor Castle, seated full length as St Agnes (Oliver Millar, *The Tudor, Stuart and Early Georgian Pictures in the Collection of Her Majesty the Queen*, London, 1963, No. 159); at Hovingham Hall, Yorks. (Sir William Worsley, Bt.), three-quarter length, facing to the right, holding flowers in her right hand, and touching a black bow on her dress with her left; in the Dartmouth collection, similar to the Hovingham portrait.

Drawing in the British Museum by Van Dyck; black chalk heightened with white, on light brown paper; $18\frac{1}{4} \times 11\frac{3}{4}$ in. 1897-8-13-3. Bibl.: & Repr.: Vey, *Die Zeichnungen Anton van Dycks*, 1962, p. 294. No. 224, Pl. 274 (not in Hind). The stance and arrangement of the drapery of the skirt are different from that which Van Dyck carried out in the portrait of her in the great family group.

164. KING CHARLES I (1600–1649)   Plate 53

Canvas, 50 × 40 in.

Three-quarter length, standing, full face, wearing armour; his right hand holds a baton, while his left rests on the helmet on a table, on which are the crown and sceptre. Plain brown background.

Cleaned in 1938. In fair condition.

Provenance: As Philip, 4th Earl of Pembroke, was Lord Chamberlain to the King, and had himself and many members of his family painted by Van Dyck between 1632 and 1635, it is probable that he asked the King's permission to have a portrait of his

Sovereign as well as one of the Queen, and of their three eldest children, and that these were done if not wholly by Van Dyck, at least in his studio and under his supervision while he was painting the numerous portraits for the King. This portrait is as good as that of the Queen is bad.

Versions: There are numerous versions of this picture.

165. QUEEN HENRIETTA MARIA (1609–1669)
Plate 54

Canvas, 50×40 in.

Youngest daughter of Henri IV of France.

Three-quarter length, standing, wearing a dark-yellow satin dress, with white lace on the bodice, shoulders and sleeves, and a black bow round the waist tied at the side. A long chain of pearls, looped in front, runs across the bodice and over the shoulders, and she wears also a pearl necklace. Her hands, one upon the other, rest rather awkwardly in front. Background of a green curtain on the right, sky in the centre, and a column on the left, below which is a table, on which rests her crown.

Cleaned, re-paints removed and repaired in 1938. Cleaning revealed damages, and much rubbing in the past, particularly in the face, hands and background. The figure is poorly drawn, and though it is contemporary with the portrait of Charles I, it would not appear that Van Dyck had much to do with its production, and probably left much of the execution to studio assistants.

Provenance: Commissioned by Philip, 4th Earl of Pembroke, about 1633.

Literature: Cust (*Van Dyck*, p. 107) says: 'On May 24th 1633, the Lord Chamberlain issued a warrant to Van Dyck to deliver his Lordship the picture of the Queen he lately made for the Lord Chamberlain' (Lord Pembroke).
It is a variation of two portraits in the Royal Collection (Oliver Millar, *op. cit.*, Nos. 147 and 168).

166. CHARLES, PRINCE OF WALES, JAMES, DUKE OF YORK, AND PRINCESS MARY, THE THREE ELDEST CHILDREN OF KING CHARLES I AND QUEEN HENRIETTA MARIA
Plate 55

Canvas, 48¾×58 in.

Full-length standing group with two King Charles spaniels; Charles, on the left, wears a yellow satin coat with slashed sleeves and a lace collar and cuffs,

breeches and stockings to match, and white shoes with yellow bows; his right arm rests on a column, and his left arm and hand is held by his brother James, dressed in white satin and lace with a lace cap on his head. Mary, on the right, is also in white satin and lace, with a little blue train to her dress, and flowers in her hair.

Inscribed on the column: REGIS MAGNAE BRIT-ANIAE PROLES PRINCEPS CAROLVS NATVS 29 MAY 1630. IACOBVS DVX EBORACENCIS NATVS 14 OCT: 1633. ET FILIA PRINCEPS MARIA NATA 4 NOV: 1631. On the base of the column: ANNO DOM. 1635.

Cleaned in 1932. In very good condition.

Provenance: With the other paintings by Van Dyck in the Double Cube room, this was at first in the family London house, Durham House in the Strand, and was brought to Wilton after the State rooms of the rebuilt house had been finished about 1653. The room was designed for the paintings, and the painting of the royal children is set in an elaborate frame surmounted by a crown and the Prince of Wales's feathers, all part of the decoration over the chimney. The 4th Lord Pembroke, who, after Charles I, was Van Dyck's principal patron, would not have been content with a mere studio painting or copy, so it is reasonable to assume that, after Van Dyck had finished the King's picture, he commissioned the artist to paint an exactly similar one for himself.
Mr Oliver Millar, discussing this painting in *The Tudor, Stuart and Early Georgian Pictures in the Royal Collection*, Phaidon Press, 1963 (No. 151, page 98), gives a most interesting history of the original, as well as of others ordered by the Queen. As he says, it was a popular design, and many versions exist in English houses and in Galleries abroad. Neither Gambarini nor Vertue, who both went to Wilton in 1731, mention it, but the reason for this is that it had probably been taken down for repairs and cleaning, and the gap it made could not be filled by any other picture. It was back in its place by 1751, when Richard Cowdry made his catalogue.

Versions: Apart from the original at Windsor Castle, there are versions at Euston Hall, Breamore, Kingston Lacy, Boughton, Grimsthorpe, Stourhead, Goodwood, Longleat, Penn, Lacock Abbey, Burton Constable, and at Dresden, and in the Metropolitan Museum of Art, New York.
Margaret, Countess of Suffolk and Berkshire. (Signed and dated.)

167. THE EARL AND COUNTESS OF BEDFORD
(1613–1700 and 1615–1684)   *Plate 58*

Canvas, 51 × 59 in.

Three-quarter length, both seated, facing, the heads turned slightly inwards. Lord Bedford, on the right, is dressed in black, with white sleeves and lace collar. The Riband of the Order of the Bath is across the dress. With his right hand, he holds the left hand of his wife, who wears a low-cut orange dress, the bodice laced with pearls; pearl ear-rings and necklace are her ornaments. In her right hand she holds a small bunch of flowers. Background of black curtain and sky.

Cleaned in 1935. In very good condition.

William Russell, 5th Earl of Bedford, son of the 4th Earl, was born in 1613; he was made a Knight of the Bath in 1626, and married in 1637 Anne Carr, daughter of Robert Carr, Earl of Somerset, and succeeded his father in 1641. He fought on both sides in the Civil War. Charles II created him a Knight of the Garter, and in 1694 he was made Marquis of Tavistock, and Duke of Bedford. He died in 1700.

Provenance: Acquired before 1730, probably in the seventeenth century. It may have been commissioned by or belonged to Anne Clifford, Countess of Pembroke, wife of the 4th Earl, as Lord Bedford was her cousin, and when she left Wilton in the 1640s for her estates in the north, decided that it should remain with the other Van Dyck portraits in the State rooms.

Portraits: Of Lord Bedford at Woburn, and, with Lord Bristol, at Althorp; of Anne Carr: at Woburn, Althorp and Petworth.

168. THE COUNTESS OF MORTON (d. 1654) AND MRS KILLIGREW (d. 1638)   *Plate 59*

Canvas, 51 × 59 in.

Lady Morton, who is on the left, is seated, full face, nearly whole length, and wears a white satin dress, with a pearl-embroidered brown band across the bodice and over the shoulders; a pearl necklace and ear-rings, and a large brooch on her dress, are her ornaments. In her right hand she holds a rose, while other roses are lying on the dress.

Mrs Killigrew, on the right, sits sideways, her fair head turned towards the left, a pearl necklace and ear-rings like Lady Morton's being her ornaments; she wears a black dress with pink lining, and fur on the shoulders. Both her hands are held out in front

of her, as if making a chaplet of flowers. Background of rocks, trees and sky.

Cleaned in 1935 and 1963. In good condition.

Anne, daughter of Sir Edward Villiers, married Robert Douglas, Lord Dalkeith, afterwards 10th Earl of Morton, who died in 1649. She was one of Queen Henrietta Maria's most devoted Ladies of the Court, and went into exile with her, dying in 1654. She was a famous beauty, as was Mrs Killigrew, born Cecilia, daughter of Sir John Crofts. Mrs. Killigrew was a Maid of Honour to the Queen; she married Thomas Killigrew, and died in 1638.

Provenance: At Wilton before 1730; either commissioned, or bought in the seventeenth century. As in the Bedford double portrait (No. 167) the Court connexion would have been very close, and in the case of Lady Morton, there was a distant relationship between her and the Herberts through the Buckingham and Bayning families.

Versions: At Blenheim Palace; and single portraits of Lady Morton are at Althorp, and in the Hermitage Gallery, and of Mrs Killigrew in the Museum of Fine Arts, Boston, Mass., in the possession of the Duke of Buccleuch, and in the Los Angeles County Museum.

There is a double portrait at Windsor Castle (Oliver Millar, *Tudor, Stuart and Early Georgian Pictures in the Royal Collection*, No. 156) of Thomas Killigrew and William, Lord Crofts, painted in 1638, which could be a companion piece.

169. THE COUNTESS OF CASTLEHAVEN

Canvas, 50 × 40 in.

Three-quarter length, full face, wearing a red dress; her left arm holds a blue mantle which partially hides her right arm, down the side of her dress, while above her left shoulder, it appears to rise or float in the air as if caught by the wind. Ornaments of pearl necklace and ear-rings.

Cleaned, overpainted background removed, and repaired in 1937. In good condition.

Elizabeth, Countess of Castlehaven, was a daughter of the 5th Lord Chandos, and was married sometime after 1631, the year in which her future husband's father, the 2nd Earl of Castlehaven and 12th Baron Audley was executed, and his titles forfeited. Castlehaven's son James, by a new patent of June 1634, had the titles restored as 13th Baron Audley, but 1st Earl of Castlehaven. It was probably soon after this that he married, and commissioned Van Dyck to paint his wife.

The dates of her birth and death are unknown.

Provenance: At Wilton before 1730; in the 1764 edition of the James Kennedy catalogue at Wilton are notes in the handwriting of a man called Gray, probably made in the late eighteenth century, in which he says, without quoting the authority, that this painting was 'bought of the Earl of Peterborough' as was the portrait of Princess Sophia by Honthorst (No. 113). If this is true, then both paintings were acquired by the 5th or 8th Lord Pembroke in the seventeenth century.

Wilkinson made this portrait out to be the wife of the infamous 2nd Lord Castlehaven, but this cannot be so, as he was executed in 1631, and this represents a comparatively young woman, and was clearly painted in the late 1630s.

170. ELIZABETH, COUNTESS OF PETERBOROUGH (1602/3–1671)   *Plate 57*

Canvas, 87 × 54 in.

Full length, facing, wearing a grey satin dress, the top of the bodice adorned with pearls. In her right hand she holds a rose, and with her left hand she raises the dress slightly; her ornaments are pearl ear-rings and necklace. A King Charles spaniel in the left foreground gazes up at her. Background of a red curtain, a column and a landscape.

Cleaned in 1933 and in 1951. In very good condition.

Elizabeth, daughter and sole heiress of William, Lord Howard of Effingham, by Anne, daughter of the 2nd Lord St. John, married before April 7, 1621, John, 1st Earl of Peterborough.

Provenance: This painting has previously been catalogued as a portrait of Lady Isabella Rich, daughter of the Earl of Holland (Gambarini and all subsequent catalogues), and there was no reason given why she should be represented at Wilton. The sitter's real identity has been discovered by Mr Oliver Millar, who had seen at Drayton in Northamptonshire – the property of Colonel Stopford-Sackville – an identical portrait (but without the dog), which is undoubtedly of Lady Peterborough, as is the version of the head, the property of Lord Wharton, on which there is a contemporary inscription.

It has already been noted (No. 169) that the portraits of Lady Castlehaven and of Princess Sophia were

bought from the 3rd Earl of Peterborough, so it is reasonable to suppose that this was bought at the same time, though it has not been possible to trace any connexion between that family and the Herbert family. As it was presumably bought by Thomas, 8th Lord Pembroke, it is strange that he told Gambarini that the portrait was of the daughter of the Earl of Holland.

171. THE DUC D'EPERNON (1592–1661)   *Plate 60*

Wood, 12½ × 9 in.

Facing to the right, riding his charger, the Duke, bareheaded, in armour, holds the reins of the horse with his left hand, and with the right hand holds his baton against his right thigh. Very faint female figures, perhaps Victory and Fame, float above his head, over which they hold a wreath; flags and trophies are in the background, and a figure outlined to the left beside the horse holds up some object.

This brilliant little oil sketch in sepia and white, for a portrait never carried out, is exactly as Van Dyck left it.

La Valette, created Duc D'Epernon by Henri III, supported Marie de Medici against Louis XIII, and Van Dyck may have done this sketch when he was assisting Rubens to decorate the great gallery of the Luxembourg Palace in 1621 for the Queen.

The Duke D'Epernon was installed a Knight of the Garter in 1661, the year of his death.

Provenance; There is no record of its acquisition, and it is not mentioned till the Richardson catalogue of 1774, during the lifetime of the 10th Earl, but it seems unlikely that he bought it; it is more probable that, being very small, it hung in a room not shown to those who had made the earlier catalogues, or it may have been in the London house. It was probably bought by Philip, 4th Earl, or Thomas, 8th Earl, in the seventeenth century.

In the 1683 Inventory at Wilton is an entry 'old King Charles on horseback, £80.'; the position of the rider and the horse, with the exception of its head, is almost identical with the great equestrian portrait of Charles I with M. de St. Antoine at Buckingham Palace (Oliver Millar catalogue, No. 143), and wrongly described on the Bernard Baron engraving of 1741 as Charles I with the Duc D'Epernon. Whoever made the 1683 Inventory might have thought that the bearded rider was

Charles I but the equestrian portrait of Charles at Corsham Court, the property of Lord Methuen, could also be the picture referred to in the Inventory.

School of Van Dyck

172. JAMES, DUKE OF RICHMOND AND LENNOX (1612–1655)

Canvas, 87×51 in.

Full length, standing, with his legs crossed, turned slightly to the left, wearing a black suit with lace collar and cuffs, black stockings and shoes. Round his neck he has the Riband and George of the Garter. His right hand rests on the top of his cuirass, below which is the helmet and a baton. His left arm is bent over which is a cloak, with the hand on his waist above the hilt of his sword. Background of landscape and columns.

Cleaned in 1932, in 1951 and in 1964. A very poor studio picture, much rubbed and overpainted.

James Stuart was the eldest son of Esmé, Duke of Lennox, first cousin once removed to James I of England, who brought him up at Court after his father had died, when he was twelve. In 1637 he married the Duke of Buckingham's daughter, Mary Villiers, widow of Charles Lord Herbert, eldest son of Philip, 4th Earl of Pembroke, and they had a son and a daughter. A great favourite of King Charles I, who created him Duke of Richmond in 1641, he remained loyal to the King in the Civil War, and is said to have died of grief in 1655.

Provenance: Probably bought by Philip, 4th Earl of Pembroke, or his son, as a pair to the portrait of Mary Villiers, painted as Duchess of Richmond with Mrs Gibson (No. 163).

173. THE INFANT CHRIST

Canvas, 18½×23 in.

The naked Child lies on His back, the head tilted so that He looks up; the left arm is across His chest and the legs are crossed. Below Him is a white drapery, part of which covers His loins. The straw-covered cradle, on which He lies, runs diagonally across the canvas, and above is a cloudy sky.

Cleaned in 1936. In good condition.

Provenance: First recorded in the Cowdry catalogue of 1751 as by Van Dyck; probably bought by Henry, 9th Earl of Pembroke.

David Teniers the Younger
1610–1690

Born in Antwerp; studied under his father, and was influenced by Brouwer and by Rubens, whose friend he was. Moved in 1650 to Brussels, where he died.

174. THE PIPE SMOKER   *Plate* 63

Wood, 8½×11¼ in.

A man in a blue coat and wearing a red cap, is seated, smoking a pipe, and holding a bowl; near his right arm is a stool on which is a white cloth and a jug. In the background on the left are five men seated, playing cards.

Signed to the left of the white cloth: D. TENIERS.F.

Cleaned in 1935 and in 1958. In very good condition.

The painting is on an oval oak panel, which has been inserted into a square panel, perhaps when it was bought by the Goldsworthy family, or after it came to Wilton; the present frame, which has an oval 'mask' inside the square, appears to date from the eighteenth century.

Provenance: One of the seven pictures given by General Philip Goldsworthy to George, 11th Earl of Pembroke, at the beginning of the nineteenth century.

Frans de Vrient
? 1517–1570

Commonly known as Frans Floris, a name assumed by his great-grandfather and father, he was born in Antwerp, studied under Lambert Lombard, and then spent some years in Rome. He became a master of the Guild of St Luke at Antwerp in 1540.

175. THE LABOURS OF HERCULES

Copper on wood, each of the six panels 9×7 in.

Six of the twelve labours are represented as follows, beginning at the top left: Hercules holding up the world, the destruction of the Lernaean hydra, obtaining the mares of Diomedes, the slaughter of the Nemean lion, delivering Dejanira from the centaur Nessus, catching the stag with golden horns.

Provenance: First recorded by Gambarini (p. 65). Probably bought by Thomas, 8th Earl of Pembroke.

Artus Wolffordt
1581–1641

Born at Antwerp; painted historical subjects, mythology, and interior scenes.

176. A SERAGLIO, OR THE BATH   *Plate* 50
Wood, $22\frac{1}{2} \times 33\frac{3}{4}$ in.

Fifteen nude or semi-nude men and women with towels, basins, ewers, bottles and looking-glasses are grouped standing, sitting, and kneeling in a darkened room or hall. On the wall is a picture of the Judgement of Paris, and in a niche a statue of Diana.

Cleaned, panel repaired and keys fixed to the back in 1952. In good condition.

Provenance: At Wilton before 1730, probably bought by Thomas, 8th Earl of Pembroke.
Attributed in the eighteenth century to 'Gessi', and later to Holsteyn. Now attributed by H. Gerson and S. Gudlaugsson to Wolffordt.

Versions: State Gallery, Cassel, Germany (No. 281); Mauritshuis, The Hague; Victoria and Albert Museum, London (No. 10; Dyce Collection).

Flemish (Antwerp) ? School, XVI or early XVII Century

177. THE DEVIL TEMPTING CHRIST TO TURN STONE INTO BREAD   *Plate* 33
Wood, $15\frac{1}{2} \times 12$ in.

Christ is seated in the right foreground, wearing a blue robe, with His left arm raised. The Devil is shown as a bearded man, in a brown robe and wearing a red cap, holding a stone in his right hand. Background of ruins, rocks and trees.

Cleaned in 1952. In good condition.

Provenance: The title is taken from Gambarini's catalogue (p. 28) under the attribution of 'Paris Alfano di Perugia', saying that it came 'from the collection of Cardinal Medici'. This is also written on the back of the panel. This painter was called Orazio Alfani di Paris or di Domenico, the name of his father, under whom he studied in Perugia, where he was born about 1510, and he became the first President of the Perugia Academy. He died in Rome in 1583. But it is clearly a Flemish Mannerist painting.

Unknown, late XVII Century. Flemish (?)

178. APOLLO AND DAPHNE
Copper, $6\frac{1}{4} \times 13\frac{3}{4}$ in.

Apollo on the right, wearing a brown robe and a red cloak, and holding a bow in his left hand, pursues Daphne, also running and turning her head to look at him; she wears a white robe and a blue cloak and carries a spear in her left hand. A sketchily painted landscape with a cherub in a cloud in the top right corner. Cleaned in 1960. In fair condition.

Provenance: At Wilton before 1730. Gambarini (p. 70) gives a fairly accurate description, and says it is by 'Abraham Johnson'. It is a copy of the painting in the Louvre by the sixteenth-century Bolognese painter, Francesco Albani.

FRENCH SCHOOL

Pierre Le Bouteux
1683–1750

Portrait painter, born in Paris; recorded in London in 1739. A portrait of a Captain James Miller, a fencing master, was engraved by Scotin, and the engraving is in the British Museum. Le Bouteux died in Lille.

179. ROBERT MATHISON
Canvas, 30½ × 24 in.

Seated, full face, his head tilted slightly to the right, the fair-haired young man wears a blue coat edged with gold, and lined with red, with a white cravat and shirt, with frills at the wrist. His right arm rests on a table, pointing with his hand at a music book score which he holds with his left hand.

Cleaned in 1951. In fair condition.

Robert Mathison's name and signature occur frequently on documents and in the household account books in the Muniment Room at Wilton in the middle of the eighteenth century, but nowhere does it say what his position or employment with the Herbert family was. Judging from this painting, he might have been a music teacher or young composer patronised by Henry, 9th Lord Pembroke, or his wife. He appears to be about thirty years old.

Provenance: Bought or perhaps commissioned by Henry, 9th Earl of Pembroke. On the back of the canvas is written in black paint 'Robert Mathison. Painted by Bouteux, 1738'.

School of François Clouet
1510 ?–1572

Clouet was probably born at Tours, and in 1541 he succeeded his father, Jehan, as painter to Francis I. He was also painter to Henry II.

180. FRANCIS II AND CHARLES IX OF FRANCE
(1544–1560 and 1550–1574) *Plate 39*
Vellum on wood, 10 × 12 in. (Each vellum strip 6 in. wide.)

Francis on the left, and Charles on the right, dressed alike in white trunk hose, velvet-embroidered coat lined with fur, buff waistcoat, flat velvet cap with ostrich feather, stand almost facing each other in similar pose; each has a long sword and Charles carries a pair of gloves in his right hand. Background of dark green curtain.

Cleaned, remounted on board, and repaired in 1933. In good condition.

Francis, born at Fontainebleau, was the eldest son of Henry II and Catherine de Medici. He was married to Mary, Queen of Scots, in 1558, became King the next year, and died the year after.
Charles, the younger son (the Duke d'Orléans) succeeded his brother, but died unmarried aged twenty-four.

Provenance: At Wilton before 1730 (attributed to Zucchero). Probably bought by Thomas, 8th Earl of Pembroke.

Jacques Courtois (Il Borgognone)
1621–1676

Born at St-Hippolyte in Franche-Comté, son of an artist who taught him to draw; at the age of fifteen he went to Italy and joined the army, but after three years left to study painting under Albani and Guido Reni. He became famous for his battle-pieces.

181. BATTLE SCENE   *Plate 115*
Canvas, 20 × 37 in.

A group of cavalry is seen on a hill, with an officer on a white horse, and a standard-bearer and two trumpeters in the foreground. In the distance a battle is raging.

Cleaned in 1915. In good condition.

Provenance: At Wilton before 1730; probably bought by Thomas, 8th Earl of Pembroke.

182. BATTLE SCENE
Canvas, 20 × 37 in.

A cavalry battle is taking place, in which two armoured and plumed riders in the foreground are about to strike each other with swords, and the horses are trampling on bodies lying on the rocky ground.

Cleaned in 1915. In good condition.

Provenance: As No. 181.

School of Fontainebleau
XVI Century

183. PIETÀ

Wood, 23¼ × 22 in.

The dead Christ, whose arms are held by two cherubs, rests against the Virgin, who is seated with arms outstretched, gazing upwards. Behind her are three Crosses, on two of which the bodies are still nailed. To the right is part of a tree from which hangs a small shield on which is a monogram W or VV.

The painting is enclosed in a separate painted border with four oblong and four small square compartments; the top oblong one has trophies of fruit and vegetables, in the centre of which is a white scroll on which is written 'Mater Dei'; the bottom similarly has 'Memēto Mei'; the side oblongs contain trophies and masks.

The top right square contains the Fleur de Lys of France, the top left the three interlaced crescent moons of Diane de Poitiers, the bottom left the monogram HD, standing for Henri II and Diane, the bottom right a bow across a quiver.

Cleaned and repaired in 1935 and in 1965. In very good condition.

Provenance: At Wilton before 1730, probably bought by Thomas, 8th Earl of Pembroke. This painting is from the lost drawing by Michelangelo made for Vittoria Colonna, which was described by Condivi and engraved by Giulio Bonasoni. As the painted border indicates, the Wilton painting was in the possession of Diane de Poitiers, and probably given to her by Henri II.

Versions: Hermitage Museum, Leningrad; Borghese Gallery, Rome, attributed to Marcello Venusti; Bordeaux, Musée; Gotha, Museum.

Jules Lefebvre
1836–1912

Born at Tournan, studied in Paris and in Rome; became a popular portrait painter, especially of women. Died in Paris.

184. THE HON. LADY HERBERT (1863–1923)

Canvas, 49 × 34½ in.

Seated, full face, wearing a low white sleeveless dress. White and blue background with flowers. Signed: Jules LeFebvre. 1884.

Born Miss Lelia Wilson, youngest daughter of Richard Wilson, of New York, and a sister of Mrs Cornelius Vanderbilt, Jnr., she married in 1888 the Hon. Michael Herbert (see No. 15).

Provenance: Presumably commissioned by Mr Wilson, and given to his daughter on her marriage, or later, and on her death it passed to her eldest son, Sir Sidney Herbert, Bt., and on his death in 1939 into the Wilton Collection.

Claude Lorraine
1600–1682

Landscape painter; Claude Gellée, called Le Lorrain. He was born at Chamagne in the Vosges; about 1613 he went to Rome, where he worked and died.

185. LANDSCAPE WITH A TREE   *Plate* 114

Canvas, 17¼ × 13½ in.

A tall tree in the foreground under which are a man and some goats and cows; a hilly landscape with a river and some buildings are in the background.

Cleaned in 1933. In 1965 the canvas, which had formerly been laid on panel, was transferred to a canvas lining; blisters were secured and it was cleaned. In good condition.

Provenance: Sir Peter Lely collection (Gambarini); at Wilton before 1730, probably bought by Thomas, 8th Earl of Pembroke, at the Lely sale in 1682, where it could have been No. 73 (18½ × 15½) as by Swanevelt.

Exhibited: Royal Academy, *17th Century Art in Europe*, 1938, No. 316.

Philippe Mercier
1689–1760

Born of French parents in Berlin; studied at the Academy there, and then travelled. Returned to Germany in 1720, settling in Hanover, where he married. Appointed by Frederick, Prince of Wales, to be his Court Painter, he settled in England, where he achieved great success, painting family groups, musical parties and fêtes champêtres in the manner of Watteau. He died in London.

186. A MUSICAL FAMILY   *Plate* 121

Canvas, 25 × 30 in.

In the centre foreground, a young man is seated, wearing a brown dress with a white collar and stockings, and playing a guitar; sitting next to him is a young woman in a white dress with a pink and gold top, holding a rose in one hand; she is looking down at a dog asleep at his feet. Behind them stand three young women wearing white, gold, and grey dresses, and small hats, in a dancing attitude. In the right background stands another young woman in a blue and gold dress with a white apron, and seated on the ground to her left is a boy, playing a flute, wearing a gold coat and breeches, and pink stockings and a hat, and a girl is sitting beside him. In the left foreground is a young woman seated, wearing a green dress, with a large mauve flower pinned to the top; she looks at a music score, which she holds with both hands. Two small girls lean against her. Looking over her shoulder is a man wearing a blue coat and hat, with a red cloak over his right arm. Background of trees and a wooded hill.

Cleaned in 1961. In very good condition.

Provenance: At Wilton before 1730; Gambarini attributes it to Watteau, as did subsequent catalogues. Mr Martin Davies of the National Gallery, London, in 1961, gave the correct attribution to Mercier.

The figures are taken from compositions by Watteau in the Wallace Collection (left group); Waddesdon Collection (centre group); Berlin, State Museums (right group).

Nicolas Poussin
? 1594–1665

Born at Villers in Normandy, he studied under French, Flemish and Italian painters; after reaching Rome, he was influenced by Raphael, and worked in Domenichino's studio. He was back in France by 1640, and patronized by Louis XIII and Richelieu, but returned to Rome in 1642 and lived there until his death.

187. TWO PUTTI   *Plate* 113

Canvas, 14 × 11¾ in.

A sketch for the two figures on the extreme left of the *Bacchanalian Revel before a term of Pan* in the National Gallery, London (No. 62), in which paint-

ing one of the Putti holds a bowl under a bunch of grapes held up by a Bacchante.

In 1963, at the suggestion of Sir Anthony Blunt, an addition of three inches all round, perhaps added in the eighteenth century, showing the children flying a kite or a toy bird on a string, was removed; at the same time, the canvas was removed from a panel board, to which it had been fixed. It was then re-lined, and a new stretcher fixed, and cleaned after repaints had been removed.

Sir Anthony thinks that it may be a very good early copy, while Professor E. K. Waterhouse thinks it is original; Sir Anthony, however, has found that a drawing at Stockholm shows two putti alone trying to catch a butterfly, and that this theme occurs in a picture by Poussin in the Hermitage, so that it is quite possible that Poussin painted a small picture with the two Putti alone. He adds that it is rare but not unknown for Poussin to repeat a single item in a bigger picture, like the kneeling satyr in another small painting in the Hermitage, which reappears exactly in the *Youth of Bacchus* at Chantilly. In two paintings in the Alte Pinakothek in Munich, the Putti are rather coarsely drawn and painted as they are in this oil sketch at Wilton.

Provenance: At Wilton before 1730, probably bought by Thomas, 8th Earl of Pembroke.

Literature: Anthony Blunt, *The Paintings of Nicolas Poussin, A Critical Catalogue*, London 1966, p. 102, No. 141.

Gaspar Poussin
1615–1675

Landscape painter. Born Gaspar Dughet, he adopted the name of his brother-in-law Nicolas Poussin, under whom he studied, and he was also influenced by Claude. He lived and worked in Rome.

188. LANDSCAPE: HAGAR AND ISHMAEL

Canvas, 24 × 19 in.

Three figures are in the lower foreground; Hagar is seated with Ishmael, who is lying on a white cloth, while a third figure stands wearing a dress with a blue skirt, one arm outstretched. In the background is a castle on a hill, and trees are in the foreground.

Cleaned in 1933 and in 1963. In fairly good condition.

Provenance: At Wilton before 1730. Probably bought by Thomas, 8th Earl of Pembroke.

Claude-Joseph Vernet
1714–1789

Seascape painter; born at Avignon, studied under his father Antoine; worked in Rome from 1734 to 1752, and then returned to France and lived in Paris.

189. HARBOUR SCENE   *Plate 116*
Canvas, 20 × 29 in.

In the foreground, fishermen are hauling in a net, while on the right a group of three women and a man stand watching. Behind them on a hill are a castle and trees. A large ship is anchored in the bay. In the background is the harbour entrance with a lighthouse, and mountains rise in the distance.

Signed in lower left hand corner: J. Vernet F. 1755.

Cleaned in 1951. In very good condition.

Provenance: Probably bought by Henry, 10th Earl of Pembroke, during his travels abroad, shortly after it was painted. In the Wilton Collection by 1758 (Kennedy catalogue).

FRANCO-SWEDISH SCHOOL

School of Alexander Roslin
1718–1793

Roslin, born in Malmö, emigrated to France as a young man, and became a member of the Academy there in 1753. He married a French woman, and after her death, returned to Sweden, and then went to Russia, where he painted Catherine the Great and members of her Court.

190. EMPRESS CATHERINE II OF RUSSIA (1729–1796)
Canvas, 29 × 23½ in.

Full face, to the waist, with grey hair or a wig, on which is a diamond crown; she wears an ermine robe over a grey satin dress, with a frill. The immense diamond corsage of the Order of St Andrew is worn over the dress, as well as the black and brown Riband of the Order of St George.

Relined and cleaned in 1936. In good condition.

The Empress was born a Princess of Anhalt-Zerbst in Stettin. In 1745 she married Peter, son of the Empress Elizabeth, who became Czar Peter III and died in 1762.

Provenance: Left by Count Simon Woronzow to his only daughter, Catherine, second wife of George, 11th Earl of Pembroke, in 1832.

GERMAN SCHOOL

Jörg Bräu see Prew

Johann Aegidius Eckhardt
? 1710–1779

Born in Germany; settled in England about 1740, and became a pupil of Jan Baptist van Loo, whose style he imitated. He was a popular portrait painter. He died in London.

191. NORTH LUDLOW BERNARD (1705–1766)
Canvas, 45½ × 35 in.

Three-quarter length; full face with a short grey wig; he wears the scarlet tunic of a Major in the Dragoon Guards, white cravat, and a buff under-coat, crimson sash and a gold belt. The gloved right hand, with the arm bent, holds the other glove against his hip; the left hand is on his sword hilt. A faint background of sky.

Re-lined and cleaned in 1965. In good condition.

For Bernard, see No. 93.

Provenance: Probably left to the Wilton Collection by the sitter's widow, Mary, whose first husband was the 9th Earl.

First mentioned in the Richardson catalogue (1774) as by 'Eccard'.

School of Hans Holbein the Younger

Hans Holbein the younger (1497/8–1543) was the younger son of his father of the same name, under whom he trained. He was born at Augsburg, but by 1515 was at Basle, where he became a member of the painters' guild in 1519. Two years earlier he had been at Lucerne, and visited northern Italy, and in 1524 he visited France. He went to London in 1526, returned to Basle in 1528, and finally settled in London in Henry VIII's service in 1532, paying short visits to France, Brussels, and Basle during the eleven years before his death in 1543.

He was a painter and draughtsman, and also designed jewelry, some buildings, and fresco decorations.

192. KING EDWARD VI (1537–1553)   *Plate 40*
Wood, 15½ × 12¼ in.

Head and shoulders, profile, facing to the left. On his head, he wears a black flat cap, embroidered with gold, from which a white ostrich feather protrudes over his light brown hair; a white lace shirt just shows round his neck, under the black and gold-embroidered jacket, over which is a dull-red coat slashed with white, and with an ermine collar. He holds a small red rose in his left hand, turned upwards. Background a plain grey.

Only son of King Henry VIII and Jane Seymour; succeeded in 1547.

Cleaned, blisters secured, and repaired in 1934. In 1963, as the panel had become badly warped, the old battens were removed from the back, and wooden keys put in place, some small cracks and paints damages were filled in, and it was surface-cleaned.

Provenance: First recorded by Gambarini (p. 63), as by Holbein it is very closely allied to the sketch at Windsor Castle, once thought to be by Holbein but now considered to be the work of an unknown artist. If the Wilton painting was done from life, and is not a sixteenth-century copy of a lost original, it may have been painted shortly before the King paid a visit to Wilton in 1552, and given to the 1st Earl of Pembroke, one of the Guardians of the boy King, who would then have been fifteen years old, which is about the age he looks.

Versions: Victoria and Albert Museum (Jones Collection) and at Woburn Abbey (Duke of Bedford), both very similar; National Portrait Gallery (No. 442). Syon House (Duke of Northumberland), identical, on canvas, seventeenth century.

Martin Maingaud
? 1660–? 1725

Portrait and history painter; was in the service of Max Emmanuel, Elector of Bavaria, 1692–1706, and later worked for the English Royal Family in Hanover.

193. FREDERICK, PRINCE OF WALES, PRINCESS
ANNE (THE PRINCESS ROYAL), PRINCESS AMELIA
SOPHIA ELEANOR, AND PRINCESS CAROLINE
ELIZABETH   *Plate* 119

Canvas, 48×37½ in.

Three-quarter length, with Princess Anne on the
right, full face, with flowers in her hair, wearing a
low-cut green dress, with lace edging; part of an
ermine robe is showing. Her left arm is bent, the
hand holding a fan resting on a ledge draped in red;
her right arm is extended, the hand holding a gold
chain, from which hang miniatures of her parents
and her grandfather. Next to her standing sideways, the head turned to the right, is the Prince of
Wales, wearing a grey wig, white lace cravat and
red coat. Next to him is Princess Amelia, full face,
wearing a low-cut brown and green dress with lace
edge. She points to her eldest sister with her right
hand across her. By her side is Princess Caroline, her
head tilted slightly up, with a red rose in her hair;
she turns towards the others, wearing a brown dress
edged with lace, and her left hand rests on some
fruit and a bunch of flowers resting on the ledge.
They seem to be looking out from behind a box or
balustrade, with a large urn behind on the left, a red
curtain on the right, and a faint wooded landscape
and some sky behind.

Cleaned and relined in 1965. In fair condition.

Frederick, Prince of Wales, born in 1707, was the
eldest son of George II, married in 1736 Princess
Augusta of Saxe-Gotha, and died in 1751. Princess
Anne, born in 1709, married in 1734 William,
Prince of Orange, and died in 1759. Princess Amelia
was born in 1711 and died unmarried in 1786.
Princess Caroline was born in 1713, and died un-
married in 1757.

Provenance: First recorded in the Richardson
catalogue (1774) as by 'Zimmen' (Seeman); now
identified as by Maingaud by Mr Oliver Millar,
who dates the painting about 1720, the same time as
the three paintings of these children in the Royal
Collection (Nos. 514–16. Oliver Millar catalogue).
Probably bought by Henry, 10th Earl of Pembroke,
or perhaps given to him or Lady Pembroke by
George III.

Jörg Prew (Bräu)

c. 1475–1537

Born in Augsburg; painted battle and historical
scenes.

193-a. 'THE BATTLE OF PAVIA'

Wood, 12×25¼ in.

Soldiers and horses are seen in their tented camps,
while the opposing armies are fighting on the
bridges over the river encircling the walls of the
city, which lies in a plain with a line of mountains in
the background.

The battle, in 1525, ended in the victory of Charles V
over the French army under Francis I, after a long
siege.

Provenance: At Wilton before 1730; Gambarini (p.
63) attributes it to Hans Holbein the Younger, and
on the back of the panel is painted in black, 'Ex Col:
Arund: Hans Holben. P.' in an eighteenth century
hand. Bought by Thomas, 8th Earl of Pembroke.

South German School, c. 1500

194. THE ENTOMBMENT   *Plate* 36

Wood, 25½×18¼ in.

The Virgin, in a blue robe with a white hood, kneels
supporting the dead Christ. Three richly robed men
stand at His head, one takes some of the weight
on his knees; Mary Magdalen kneels and wipes His
feet, and to her right another woman in blue kneels
and looks up to the right and gesticulates at a white-
bearded man and two younger men holding nails,
pincers, and hammer. A red-robed figure, probably
St John, kneels and prays behind Christ and the
Virgin. In the centre background five figures are
grouped around the open tomb, while two more
come down a path by the rocks on the left. A multitude of small figures are seen in the distant hilly
landscape, and on the hill of Calvary to the right are
the Crosses with more small figures.

Cleaned in 1930 and in 1965. By 1964 the panel had
become badly warped; by taking off (or reducing)
the thickness of the panel, which was then placed in
a moist atmosphere and weighted down for two
months, the curvature was eliminated without any
damage to the paint, which except for an old small
crack down the centre, is in very good condition. It
has now been strengthened by re-backing it with
balsa wood.

Provenance: At Wilton before 1730; Gambarini calls
it 'Albert Durer, he has placed a Monogram of his
name on the picture, which was one of the Arundell
Collection'. When the picture was cleaned, the false
AD monogram over the door of the tomb came off

easily. All subsequent eighteenth-century catalogues called it Dürer. Passavant in 1833 attributed it to a painter called 'Jarenus' because this word appears on the tablet held by one of the men on the left, but it is merely part of the inscription which, if fully shown, would read 'Jesus Nazarenus'. Waagen in 1835 fell into the same trap. Woltmann in 1879, in the 'Repertorium für Kunstwissenschaft' points out the error and attributes it to a painter of the Lower Rhine under Netherlands influence. Friedländer attributed it to a Nuremberg Master of the Franconian School; Dr W. Houben (1948) and Mr Martin Davies both to the South German School, about 1500.

Wilhelm von Kaulbach
1805–1874

Born at Arolsen, studied under his father, and in Düsseldorf. In 1825 he went to Munich, becoming Director of the Academy there in 1847.

195. FIELD MARSHAL PRINCE MICHAEL WORONZOW (1782–1856)

Canvas, 48 × 36 in.

Three-quarter length, standing, full face, with white hair and side-whiskers, wearing a dark-blue uniform piped with red, with gold epaulettes and aiguillettes and sword belt. His hands are crossed in front, the sword hilt showing behind a sleeve. On his left breast are the Stars of three Russian Orders, and above are medals and other Orders are suspended from his neck. Background of sky and the Caucasus Mountains.

Cleaned in 1950. In good condition.

For details of Prince Woronzow, see No. 30.

Painted when in his sixties or later, about 1845.

Provenance: Probably left by the sitter to his sister, Lady Pembroke, who died the same year, which may account for its omission from her lists of possessions left by her to her son, Sidney Herbert, whose wife included it in a list as 'By a Berlin Artist, left to Lord Herbert by his Mother'.

Versions: At Abbey Leix, Ireland (Lord De Vesci): better quality, and probably the original. One of Catherine Lady Pembroke's daughters, Emma, married Lord De Vesci.

German School, XVIII Century

196. FERDINAND, DUKE OF BRUNSWICK AND LUNEBURG, K.G. (1721–1792)

Canvas, oval, 22 × 17¾ in.

Head and shoulders, full face, head turned slightly towards his left; he has white hair (or wears a thin white wig), and is in a blue and yellow uniform, with a black and white cravat. The only Order is that of the Garter, Star and Riband.

Cleaned in 1955.

On the back of the frame is an old metal label which says that he was born 'Ye 12th January 1721', but the Peerage gives the year of his birth as 1735. The label also says 'from a picture done in 1760', and in the portrait he is certainly an elderly man, which he would not have been if he was born in 1735.

It is a poor copy of a painting at Windsor Castle.

Provenance: Probably bought by Henry, 10th Earl of Pembroke, whose friend the sitter was.

ITALIAN SCHOOL

Niccolò dell'Abbate

1509–1571

Studied under his father, Giovanni, as well as Correggio; worked in Modena, Bologna, and in France, where he died.

197. THE DEPOSITION

Wood, $10\frac{3}{4} \times 9$ in.

The dead Christ is supported by angels at His head and feet, and four other figures stand behind in attitudes of despair.

A very slight oil sketch.

Provenance: At Wilton before 1730; Gambarini (p. 36) says 'Bonamico Bufalmaco, a Dead Christ, in black and white'.

Pompeo Batoni

1708–1787

Born at Lucca; studied in Rome under Sebastiano Conca. Known chiefly as a portrait painter. Lived and died in Rome.

198. HENRY, IOTH EARL OF PEMBROKE (1734–1794) *Plate 16*

Canvas, 39×29 in.

Three-quarter length, turned slightly to his left; he stands with his right arm resting on the base of a column. His left arm, under which is his cocked hat, is bent so that his hand is round the neck of a brown dog, who looks up at him, and whose front paws rest against his scarlet, blue and gold tunic of a cornet in the 1st Royal Dragoons. Round his neck is a black and white cravat. Background of a column on the left, and drapery on the right.

Re-lined, repaired and cleaned in 1950. In good condition.

Provenance: Painted in Rome when Lord Pembroke was on the Grand Tour in 1754, aged 20.

199. GEORGE, LORD HERBERT (1759–1827) *Plate 26*

Canvas, oval, $27\frac{1}{2} \times 22$ in.

Turned half to the right, to the waist, powdered hair, wearing a black necktie, white cravat, scarlet coat with blue collar of a cornet in the 15th Light Dragoons (Eliot's Light Horse). His right arm is bent across the bottom of the picture, and his left hand buttons up the buff waistcoat across his chest.

For details of Lord Herbert, afterwards 11th Earl of Pembroke, see No. 62.

Provenance: Commissioned by Lord Herbert. Signed near his left hand: 'POMPEO DE BATONI. Pinx. ROMA. 1779.'

This painting is at present in the possession of the Hon. David Herbert; it belonged formerly to the late Sir Sidney Herbert, Bt., who inherited it from his aunt Lady Mary von Hugel, a grand-daughter of the sitter.

Reproduced: Henry, Elizabeth and George, The Pembroke Papers, 1939, edited by Lord Herbert.

After Pompeo Batoni

200. GEORGIANA, COUNTESS SPENCER (1737–1814)

Canvas, $22 \times 17\frac{1}{4}$ in.

Head and shoulders, full face, turned slightly to her left, with a white lace frill round her neck, and wearing a low-cut brown dress edged with white.

Cleaned in 1951. In good condition.

Georgiana, daughter of Stephen Poyntz, of Midgham, Berks, married John, 1st Earl Spencer, in 1755.

Provenance: On the back of the canvas is written 'Given to the Wilton Collection of paintings by Elizabeth, Countess Dowager of Pembroke and Montgomery in June 1828'. Lady Pembroke, born a Spencer, was a cousin of Georgiana's husband.

Professor E. K. Waterhouse has pointed out that this is a copy, of the head only, of a three-quarter length portrait, signed by Pompeo Batoni and dated 1764, in the possession of Earl Spencer at Althorp, and that a similar copy was formerly at Mount Browne.

Paulus Bril
1554–1626

Born in Antwerp, but emigrated at an early age to Rome, where he died.

201. LANDSCAPE

Canvas, 19×24 in.

A high rocky island near the shore, on and near which are men and boats.

Cleaned in 1952. In fairly good condition.

Provenance: In the Gambarini catalogue as by Bril, 'a landskep, with a rocky island in the middle of the sea, with boats and men standing on the shore'. Probably bought by Thomas, 8th Earl of Pembroke.

Luca Cambiaso
1527–1585

Born at Moneglia near Genoa; he was known as Luchetto da Genova, and was instructed by his father, and influenced by Castelli. He visited Rome and Florence, and then went to Spain, where he worked for Philip II, and died there.

202. CHRIST IN THE CARPENTER'S SHOP

Wood, 11½×10 in.

Christ, in a red coat over a white shirt, stands leaning with His left arm against the work bench, while in His right hand He holds an oil lamp lighting up the carpenter at work; the latter wears a white and brown dress, and a scarf covering the lower half of his face, while on his head is a kind of brown helmet, In the background, descending the stairs and holding another oil lamp, is the Virgin Mary.

Cleaned in 1933. In good condition.

Provenance: At Wilton before 1730; probably bought by Thomas, 8th Earl of Pembroke.

Michelangelo Cerquozzi
1602–1660

Sometimes known as Michelangelo delle Battaglie. Born in Rome, studied in the School of Bonzi (Il Gobbo da Cortona), and later under de Laer. He painted a variety of subjects, landscapes, fairs, battle-pieces, flowers and fruit, and sometimes had other painters to collaborate with him, and in this case, according to Gambarini, it was Viviano Codazzo.

203. LANDSCAPE WITH FIGURES *Plate 97*

Canvas, 26×19½ in.

A group of four men, two seated and two standing, are seen in the lower left foreground, a woman is in the middle, and a donkey on the right, under a ruined arch, through which is seen a river or lake, with a town or village beyond with classical and Byzantine churches, and towers and houses. Behind is a hill and the sky.

Repaired and cleaned in 1960. In good condition.

Provenance: At Wilton before 1730; probably bought by Thomas, 8th Earl of Pembroke. According to Gambarini (p. 21) one of a pair: 'A summer piece (being an exact pair). Ruins with figures. Viviano Codazzo and Mich. Angelo delle Battaglie'. The other, no longer at Wilton, is described as 'a Winter piece, Ruins, with figures throwing snowballs'.

Pietro Berettini da Cortona
1596–1669

Born at Cortona; instructed by his uncle, Filippo Berettini, and later by Commodi and Ciarpi. He worked mainly in Rome, paying visits to Florence and Venice.

204. THE RAPE OF THE SABINES *Plate 98*

Canvas, 45×67½ in.

Fifteen figures of women, children and Roman soldiers are struggling in the foreground; in the centre background are more smaller figures shown against trees and sky, while on the left is a statue and a column, and on the right is a classical temple.

Cleaned in 1964. In good condition.

Provenance: At Wilton before 1730; probably bought by Thomas, 8th Earl of Pembroke. Gambarini (p. 44) says: 'It was a present to Card: Mazarin, and is the first Model of the great one at Rome, that has be grav'd; the Duke of Marlborough has the fine copy which was made for a French Ambassador'. Wilkinson in Appendix IV mentions this painting as being in Herbert House, Belgrave Square, London, in 1907.

Giuseppe Maria Crespi

1665–1747

Born in Bologna; studied under various painters, Canuti, Cignani, and Burini. He visited Venice, Parma, and other northern towns, and modelled his style after Pietro da Cortona, Barocci and Guercino.

205. A GROUP OF MARKET PEOPLE   *Plate* 109

Canvas, 17 × 13 in.

In the centre is a white horse, on which sit a woman and a child; to the right are two other women, one carrying a basket on her shoulder, while in the foreground, below the horse, a man kneels over a large basket, into which he puts his right hand. To the left a girl leans on a donkey.

Cleaned in 1933. In good condition.

Provenance: At Wilton before 1730; probably bought by Thomas, 8th Earl of Pembroke.

? Girolamo Donnini

1681–1743

Born at Correggio; studied under Francesco Stringa, and later at Forlì under Carlo Cignani.

206. CUPIDS PLAYING BLIND MAN'S BUFF

Copper, 13½ × 17¾ in.

Seven cupids, one blindfolded, are playing near a small fountain on the right; an obelisk is on the left in a landscape background.

Cleaned in 1950.

A very feeble painting by an obscure artist.

Provenance: At Wilton before 1730; Gambarini (p. 31), 'boys at play, one is blinded'.

Francesco Grimaldi

1606–1680

Called Il Bolognese, he studied under Carracci. He achieved fame in Rome, where he worked for the Popes, and in 1648 went to France, where he worked for Mazarin and Louis XIV. Later he returned to Rome, where he died.

207. LANDSCAPE

Canvas, 19¼ × 25½ in.

A man carrying a fishing-net walks in the foreground to the right towards a lake or pond in a wooded landscape.

Re-lined and cleaned in 1932, and in 1966. In very good condition.

Provenance: At Wilton before 1730, probably bought by Thomas, 8th Earl of Pembroke; it may have been in the Mazarin collection.

Lorenzo Lotto

? 1480–1556

Probably born in Venice; worked in Treviso, Bergamo, Ancona, Loreto, and Rome. Influenced by Giovanni Bellini.

208. ST ANTHONY THE HERMIT   *Plate* 82

Wood, 13½ × 15¾ in.

St Anthony sits on the ground reclining against a flat-topped rock, over which is suspended a bell; the bearded figure wears a blue robe with a very wide white collar. He is inside a grotto and points to the world without with the thumb of his right hand, while his left arm rests on the rock and the hand is stretched out. A distant landscape of trees and hills is seen through the opening of the grotto.

Cleaned, re-paints removed and repaired in 1933.

The panel had become warped and was in danger of splitting, so in 1965 more than half the thickness of the panel was shaved away, then flattened and backed by balsa wood.

Provenance: At Wilton before 1730, probably bought by Thomas, 8th Earl of Pembroke.

Exhibited: Royal Academy, London, 1950–51 (Holbein and other Masters of the sixteenth and seventeenth centuries, No. 219).

Literature: Bernard Berenson, *Lorenzo Lotto* (Phaidon Press, 1956, p. 85, and plate 267), in which he says: 'The large head of the Saint is almost certainly a portrait. The action recalls the Madonna in the Uffizi picture. The technique and the folds of the draperies are of this precise period. The landscape – the charming part of the picture – differs little from the one in the *Holy Family* at Bergamo of 1533, and even less from a work of slightly later date, the

Louvre *Recognition of the Holy Child'*. Berenson dates the Wilton painting to 1534, not earlier.

Bernard Berenson, *Italian Pictures of the Renaissance, Venetian School* (Phaidon Press, 1957, vol. I, p. 107). S. A. Strong in *Art Journal*, 1899, p. 93, wrongly attributed it to Moretto da Brescia.

209. THE ASSUMPTION OF THE VIRGIN *Plate* 81

Wood, 10 × 21¾ in.

The Virgin rises, accompanied by cherubs. In the landscape below, eleven of the Apostles in various attitudes expressive of ecstasy, gaze and yearn towards her; on the hillside the twelfth Apostle runs to join them.

Cleaned in 1934. In very good condition.

Provenance: At Wilton before 1730, probably bought by Thomas, 8th Earl of Pembroke.

Literature: Bernard Berenson (*Lorenzo Lotto*, Phaidon Press, 1956, p. 26) says that this is a studio version of the panel (from the predella of the Recanati *Transfiguration* of 1512) in the Brera Gallery, Milan.

Alessandro Magnasco

1667–1749

Born in Genoa; he studied at Milan under Filippo Abbiati, specialising in Landscapes.

210. LANDSCAPE WITH FIGURES

Canvas, 27 × 22½ in.

Three small figures are seen seated or lying in a wild and dark wooded landscape.

Cleaned in 1936. In fair condition.

Provenance: Not traced in the Gambarini catalogue, and therefore probably bought by the 9th or the 10th Earl after 1733.

Francesco Mazzuola

1504–1540

Called Il Parmegianino, he was born in Parma, and studied under his uncles Michel and Pier Ilario, but soon came under the influence of Correggio. After travelling to Rome, he met and was greatly helped by Raphael and Michelangelo, and received many commissions for churches; some of his frescoes as well as numerous altar-pieces in Rome, Bologna and Parma have survived, and he is represented by paintings of religious subjects in most Galleries of Europe.

211. THE VIRGIN AND CHILD WITH ST JOHN AND ST CATHERINE

Wood, 31½ × 23½ in.

The Virgin, dressed in a pale green-blue robe, is seated on the right, gazing at the naked infant Christ, who stands at her knees; her right hand holds His left arm. He is kissing St John, who stands beside Him, and behind them St Catherine is seated, looking towards the Virgin. Background of a wooded landscape, and in the top left-hand corner, appearing out of a cloud, is a half-naked figure.

Cleaned and repaired in 1966. The panel had warped badly, but is now almost perfectly flat, and this was achieved without in any way reducing the thickness of the wood, or altering the supports at the bottom and top at the back where, a long time ago, horizontal splits in the panel had occurred two inches and one inch in depth respectively, and had been rejoined to the main panel.

The drawing and painting is typical of Parmegianino's style, and is somewhat coarse.

Provenance: One of the eight paintings presented by Cosimo III to Philip, 5th Earl of Pembroke; written on the back in a much later hand, with black paint is the inscription: 'Il dono dil Gran: Duca da Fio: a Filip; Com: di Pembr: Francesco Parmiggiano. P.'.

Versions: There are paintings of this composition in Galleries in Italy, and formerly at Hopetoun House, Scotland, the property of the Marquess of Linlithgow, an exactly similar painting, better drawn and more brilliant in execution.

Pier Francesco Mola

1612–1666

Born at Coldrerio near Como, studied under Cesari d'Arpino and Orsi in Rome, and also in Bologna and Venice. He worked mainly in Rome, where he died.

212. BACCHUS AND ARIADNE   *Plate* 100

Canvas, 19½ × 26 in.

Bacchus, seated on a rock in a landscape, talks to Ariadne, who is facing him, also seated. His arms and legs are bare; red and white drapery covers his body, and on his head is a wreath, and in his left hand is a long pole. Ariadne wears a black dress cut square at the neck, with white puffed sleeves.

Cleaned in 1951. In good condition.

The figures are taken straight from the Bridgewater Titian, *The three ages of Man* (in the collection of the Duke of Sutherland), which Mola must have seen when it was in the possession of Queen Christina of Sweden, soon after 1650.

Provenance: At Wilton before 1730, probably bought by Thomas, 8th Earl of Pembroke.

Versions: Herzog Anton Ulrich Museum, Brunswick (No. 137). This is considerably larger than the Wilton painting, which appears to have been cut down in size (as only Bacchus's knees are showing and half the trees and sky have been cut off) unless it is a reduced 'sketch' for the Brunswick painting.

Exhibited: Royal Academy, *17th Century Art in Europe*, 1938, No. 310.

Jacopo Palma (Il Giovane)
1544–1628

Son of Antonio, and great-nephew of Palma Vecchio; instructed by his father, but after going to Rome, studied Caravaggio; returning to his native town, Venice, he worked there for the rest of his life.

213. SOLDIERS DISPUTING OVER CHRIST'S GAR-
MENTS   *Plate* 93

Canvas, 51 × 60 in.

Four life-size figures, wearing brown tunics or robes, and armour, one with a red hat and another with a helmet, fight each other and tear at the garments.

Cleaned in 1933. In good condition. Painted on a very coarse canvas. Possibly a fragment of a much larger painting.

Provenance: At Wilton before 1730, when Gambarini ascribes it to Annibale Carracci, and says it belonged to Monsieur Fouquet, who died in 1680, so it was bought soon after by Thomas, 8th Earl of Pembroke.

Gian Paolo Panini
? 1691–1764

Born at Piacenza; he studied at Rome under Locatelli and Luti; known chiefly for views of ruins, monuments, and interiors.

214. RUINS WITH FIGURES   *Plate* 111

Canvas, 15 × 11 in.

Four figures are seen seated and standing among broken columns and fallen stones.

Cleaned in 1933. In good condition.

Provenance: At Wilton before 1730. Probably bought by Thomas, 8th Earl of Pembroke.

Literature: G. P. *Panini*, a cura di F. Arisi (Cassa di Risparmio di Piacenza), 1961, Pl. 65; scheda n. 39 (c. 1720).

Gianfrancesco Penni
1488–1528

Called Il Fattore, he was born in Florence; apprenticed to Raphael in Rome as a young man, he became his principal pupil, assistant and copyist, and painted a number of religious subjects, landscapes and frescoes, before he died at the early age of 40.

215. THE HOLY FAMILY WITH THE LAMB *Plate* 83

Wood, 11 × 8½ in.

The Virgin, wearing a red and blue dress, with Joseph in blue and brown, leaning on his staff behind her, holds the infant Christ, who is seated on a lamb at her feet. Background of rocky hills with buildings and trees.

Cleaned, broken panel repaired and cradled in 1934. In fair condition.

Provenance: At Wilton before 1730, correctly attributed. Probably bought by Thomas, 8th Earl of Pembroke.

Versions: Sold at Christie's, November 25, 1966, No. 18, for 4000 guineas (ex Lord Lee of Fareham collection). There are other copies in European Galleries after Raphael's masterpiece of 1507 in the Prado, Madrid, No. 296.

Giuseppe Porta (Il Salviati)
1520 ?–1580 ?

Born at Castel Nuovo in the Garfagnana; went to Rome to study under Francesco Rossi, and then worked in Venice, Padua and Rome before returning to Venice, where he died.

216. CHRIST IN THE TEMPLE

Paper on wood; pen and sepia heightened with oil, 12×7½ in.

Christ stands turned to the right, with His right arm outstretched, on the top of three steps, with six or seven figures grouped behind Him and two more reclining in front below the desk in front of Him.

Provenance: First recorded in the Richardson catalogue, 1774 (p. 43), as by Salviati; probably bought by the 10th Earl. On the corner of the lower step is stamped in black PL (from the Lely collection, and not PHL. as Wilkinson says meaning Philip Liefrinck), and an eight-pointed star, which he says is the mark of the Arundel collection. Wilkinson also says that this is 'Merely a woodcut on paper mounted on panel'.

Giovanni Francesco Romanelli
1610–1662

Born at Viterbo; studied under Pietro da Cortona in Rome, where he established a reputation which brought him much work, particularly for the Church. He visited France, where Mazarin employed him; he died in Viterbo.

217. HARMONY BETWEEN HISTORY AND POETRY

Canvas, 51¼×38 in.

Two three-quarter length allegorical female figures, one with a pen and a book, the other writing with a pen, face each other; between them, in a blue sky, is a putto with a trumpet, and a snake eating its own tail (symbols of Fame and Eternity). Left background is the base of the column of Trajan.
Probably painted after 1644.

Cleaned in 1937. In good condition.

Provenance: In the Wilton Collection before 1730.

Version: Coombe Priory, Shaftesbury, Dorset (Mr T. Hetherington).

Exhibited: Royal Academy, 17th Century Art in Europe, 1938, No. 300.

Jacopo Robusti (Il Tintoretto)
1518–1594

Thought to have studied under Titian, Bonifazio, Schiavone and others. Lived and worked in Venice.

218. CHRIST WASHING THE DISCIPLES' FEET
Plates 91, 92, 94

Canvas, 58×99 in.

Christ kneels in the right foreground with His left arm on a large copper bowl; St Peter, standing between two other disciples, has his right foot on the bowl. In the left foreground one disciple, who is seated, is pulling off the stocking of another; a dog links the figures in the left and right foreground. In the left background, two more disciples are seated in a dark corner, reading, while Judas stands against a column, a solitary figure in red; behind him are buildings and the sky. In the centre of the composition are four more disciples seated, reading at a table, underneath which is a cat. In the right background is a girl in white, sweeping the kitchen floor.

Painted about 1535.

Cleaned, some small damages repaired, a later addition to the top removed, and new strainer supplied in 1932. In perfect condition.

Provenance: At Wilton before 1730; a Tintoretto was in the collection of Philip, 4th Earl, about 1650, according to the List made of the contents of Durham House at that time (see Introduction) and it may therefore be this painting. If not, it was acquired by Thomas, 8th Earl.

Versions: Prado, Madrid; National Gallery, London (1130); Venice, San Moisé; Venice, Santo Stefano; National Gallery of Canada, Ottawa (ex Farnham coll: 1959).

Literature: Tancred Borenius in *The Burlington Magazine*, Vol. 61 (1932); Bernard Berenson, *Italian Pictures of the Renaissance, Venetian School* (Phaidon Press, 1957), Vol. I, p. 183; Vol. II, pl. 1272.

Salvator Rosa
1615–1673

Born at Renella near Naples. During an adventurous and difficult life, he had few friends or masters. He worked mainly in Rome, Naples and Florence. He died in Rome.

219. LANDSCAPE WITH FIGURES   *Plate* 99

Canvas, 19×25½ in.

A hilly and rocky landscape with a waterfall forming in the right foreground a little pond, on which are two swans; three men, two seated and one standing with a long pole, are in the foreground talking.

Painted in the late 1630s.

Re-lined and cleaned in 1932. In good condition.

Provenance: At Wilton before 1730. Gambarini (p. 20), says 'Bartolomeo (imitation of S. Rosa) a Landskip with a cascade, and three Travellers talking'. Probably bought by Thomas, 8th Earl of Pembroke.

Andrea Sacchi
1599–1661

Born at Nettuno, near Rome, son of a painter, he studied under Francesco Albani.

220. JOB WITH HIS WIFE AND FRIENDS *Plate* 101

Canvas, 11×14½ in.

Job lies nearly naked, except for a red drapery, with his legs crossed and his arms outstretched, against a ruined wall, while to the right is his wife standing, and two men, one seated, pointing and gazing at Job.

Cleaned in 1952. In good condition.

Provenance: At Wilton before 1730, probably bought by Thomas, 8th Earl of Pembroke.

Giovanni Battista Salvi
1609–1685

Born in Ancona, son of a painter. He was called Il Sassoferrato; a follower of the Carracci, and was also influenced by Domenichino. He worked mainly in Rome.

and Mario Nuzzi
1604–1673

Called MARIO DE' FIORI. Born at Penna; studied under his uncle, Tommaso Salini, a flower painter, whom he followed, working in Rome where his flower paintings were very popular.

220–a. THE MADONNA   *Plate* 102

Canvas, 29×23½ in.

The head of the Madonna, full face, looking slightly downwards, is covered with a dark blue hood, lined with white. Her hands only, in an attitude of prayer, show just below her neck. A wreath of flowers composed of tulips, carnations, roses and other flowers completely encircle her.

Cleaned in 1950. Old re-paints removed and repaired. In fair condition.

Provenance: At Wilton before 1730; Gambarini (p. 105): 'Sasso Ferati, the Virgin, the vail painted with ultra marine, which makes a most beautiful Claro oscuro. Maria di Fiori painted the flowers round the Virgin'. Bought by Thomas, 8th Earl of Pembroke.

Andrea del Sarto
1486–1530

Born Andrea d'Agnolo in Florence; after initial study under Barile, he entered the School of Piero di Cosimo. He was influenced by Ghirlandaio, Leonardo da Vinci and Michelangelo. Except for three years in Paris, he worked in Florence.

221. THE VIRGIN AND CHILD, ST JOHN, A YOUNG WOMAN AND CHILD   *Plate* 85

Wood, 41×31 in.

The Virgin wears a red and blue dress, with purple drapery on her head, and is seated, turning slightly to the right, with her left hand round Christ, who stands naked beside her, looking over His shoulder. St John, at her feet, looks over his right shoulder, and behind him is a young woman with a child, who clings to her. In the top right background in the sky is a saint and an angel.

Cleaned and repaired in 1932. In very good condition.

Provenance: One of the eight pictures given to Philip, 5th Earl of Pembroke, by the Medici Grand-

Duke Cosimo III in 1669, when he paid a visit to Wilton. On the back of the panel in black paint is written in a later hand: 'Il dono dil Gran Duca da Fior a Filip Com: di Pembr. Andrea del Sarto P.'

Versions: Wallace Collection, London; Prado, Madrid; Munich, Alte Pinakothek; Borghese Gallery, Rome; Longford Castle, Salisbury.

Andrea del Sarto
1487–1531
or
Francesco Ubertini, called Il Bacchiacca
1495–1557

222. CHRIST BEARING THE CROSS   *Plate 86*

Wood, 16¼ × 12 in.

Christ, wearing a pink robe, has fallen to His knees under the weight of the Cross, His face turned towards the spectator. To the left is a soldier with uplifted arm ready to strike Him. Background of large rocks.

Cleaned in 1933. In fairly good condition.

This seems to be a fragment of a larger painting, as the soldier is almost cut in two vertically, and may be part of a series of the story of the Crucifixion of which there are similiar small panels in the Pitti Palace in Florence, and in the National Gallery in Dublin. Mr Mostyn Owen considers that it is probably the work of Ubertini.

Provenance: Not mentioned by Gambarini in 1731, but in the Catalogue by Richard Cowdry, 1751, and therefore probably bought by Henry, 9th Earl of Pembroke.

Giovanni Girolamo Savoldo
? 1480–? 1548

Born in Brescia; he worked in Venice and was chiefly influenced by Giorgione.

223. A PIPER   *Plate 88*

Canvas, 20½ × 16 in.

Head and shoulders of a slightly bearded young man, turned towards the right, wearing a black hat, and a fur-trimmed coat. In his left hand he carries a pipe or flute.

Cleaned, old re-paints removed and repaired in 1932. Much rubbed, and the paint is very thin.

Provenance: One of the eight pictures given to Philip, 5th Earl of Pembroke, by the Grand-Duke Cosimo III in 1669 (see Introduction, p. 4) as by Giorgione, which attribution remained throughout the eighteenth and nineteenth centuries. It was correctly attributed to Savoldo by Sir Kenneth Clark in 1936.

Versions: National Gallery, Edinburgh (No. 69), as Venetian School; Bowood House, Wiltshire (Marquess of Lansdowne), erroneously called 'Antonello, Prince of Salerno'; Cini Foundation, Venice; Museo Nazionale, Naples; Historical Society, New York; Charlecote Park, England (Fairfax Lucy collection); Mr J. A. Murnaghan, Dublin (1958). Berenson listed the Cini and Bowood versions as by Sebastiano del Piombo. Yet another version ascribed to del Piombo was sold at Christie's in 1927, as a portrait of a gentleman in a blue dress with a red cloak, fur collar and black hat.

Cesare da Sesto
1477–1523

Born at Sesto Calende, and known as Cesare Milanese; he was Leonardo da Vinci's principal pupil, and much of his work is similar. He died in Milan.

224. LEDA AND THE SWAN   *Plate 84*

Wood, 38 × 29 in.

Leda stands naked, with her arms round the swan's neck, whose right wing encircles her right thigh. In the foreground, left, emerging from two eggs are Castor and Pollux and Helen and Clytemnestra. Background of a river, hills, trees and a castle.

Cleaned, blisters secured, re-paints removed in 1930; surface cleaned in 1952. In very good condition.

Provenance: In the Wilton collection before 1730. Gambarini states that it was bought from the Arundel collection, therefore by Thomas, 8th Earl of Pembroke.

Versions: Borghese Gallery, Rome (two children only); formerly Spiridon collection, Rome; John G. Johnson Collection, Philadelphia.

Exhibited: Royal Academy, *Leonardo da Vinci*

Quincentenary Exhibition, London, 1952, No. 259, and Pl. 71.

Literature: A Catalogue of the Drawings by Leonardo da Vinci at Windsor Castle, by Kenneth Clark, Cambridge, 1935, p. 77, note to 12516; Kenneth Clark, *Leonardo da Vinci*, Cambridge, 1939, p. 125 (first attribution to Cesare da Sesto) and pl. 41; A. E. Popham, *The Drawings of Leonardo da Vinci*, 1946, pp. 128 and 138, and pl. 210. Popham dates the drawing for the head in the Royal collection about 1504–6, which is identical with the head of the Leda at Wilton, and the painting, which Clark dates between 1506 and 1510, may have been begun by Leonardo and completed under his supervision in the studio by Cesare da Sesto.

Francesco Simonini
1689–1753

Born at Parma; a pupil of Ilario Spolverini. Painted battle scenes, and horses. He lived in Venice, where he died.

225. A ROMAN SOLDIER HANGING FROM THE GALLOWS AND EIGHTEEN HORSES

Canvas, 23 × 38 in.

In the centre, hanging from the gallows, is a man dressed as a Roman soldier (or Emperor); ranged on either side are nine horses on the right and eight on the left, with one above the gallows, facing. Under each horse is written in English the name of the Roman Emperors and Greek Commanders to whom they belonged, and that of Marshal Turenne's horse. Above and inside the gallows' posts is a strange mixture of Latin and English mainly dealing with Caesar and his evil character.

Below the gallows post on the right are the words 'Simonini pinxit', and on the opposite side 'Hipp invenit'.

Provenance: There is no record of the acquisition of this extraordinary painting, but it may have been bought by the 10th Earl.

Elisabetta Sirani
1638–1665

Studied under her father Giovanni Andrea Sirani; became a follower of Guido Reni. Poisoned by her maid.

226. ST MARY MAGDALEN

Canvas, 18½ × 14½ in.

Kneeling, against a background of rocks, through which is seen a distant landscape on the right; she is dressed in white with a yellow cloak over it. Her right hand clutches her long light brown hair, which falls over her neck, and her left arm is outstretched. On her right is a book and a skull on the rock. Two angels are shown against a white cloud at which she is looking up to the right.

Cleaned in 1955. In good condition.

Provenance: At Wilton before 1730; probably bought by Thomas, 8th Earl of Pembroke. Gambarini (p. 87) describes the painting as follows: Girolamo da Carpi, his manner of Corregio, a Magdalen kneeling at prayers with a book on a rock, and she has a Discipline, the light breaks in behind her; from the Arundel collection.

Tintoretto
see Robusti, No. 218

Antonio Viviani
Flourished mid-17 century

Called Codagora, he studied at the Academy at Rome. He painted landscapes, ruins and perspectives, usually in 'miniature' style.

227. HARBOUR SCENE   *Plate* 110

Copper, 11 × 21½ in.

Three large ships are at anchor, close to a pier, on which are many tiny figures; another ship is in the distance; the castellated walls, towers and houses of the town, with hills beyond, are in the right background. In the left foreground are two trees, six more figures, a dog and an anchor on a rock.

Signed in monogram AEV on the rock foreground below the man and dog.

Cleaned in 1950. In good condition.

Provenance: At Wilton before 1730; Gambarini describes it as the Port of Leghorn, but it bears no resemblance to that town, now or in the past; it is a purely imaginary composition, as were many of Viviani's works.

Francesco Zuccarelli
1702–1788

Born at Pitigliano in Tuscany. Landscape painter; he studied under Anesi in Florence and Nelli in Rome. Twice visited England, and became a foundation member of the Royal Academy. Died in Florence.

228. LANDSCAPE WITH FIGURES
Canvas, $18\frac{1}{2} \times 29$ in.

A young woman in a blue and mauve dress and a white apron, her right arm outstretched, and a basket over her left arm, is accompanied by a small child and a dog. They walk towards a stream, in which a cow and a goat are making their way to the opposite bank, which is being climbed by a young herdsman. Behind him there is a wood. In the background of hills, two of which have castles on them, the stream winds between trees and rocks, and a figure is riding on a white horse.

Cleaned and repaired in 1960. In very good condition.

Provenance: At Wilton by 1774 (Aedes Pembrochianae. By Mr Richardson) correctly attributed, but not in the earlier catalogues, and was therefore bought by Henry, 10th Earl.

Italian School (Venetian), XVII Century.
After Paolo Veronese

229. THE ADORATION OF THE MAGI
Canvas, $38 \times 28\frac{3}{4}$ in.

The Virgin, seated at the foot of a column, holds the infant Christ, and looks down at the kneeling and standing Magi. Behind her stands Joseph; other figures are in the centre and on the left, including a Negro, and a man holding a horse; they are grouped in front of the rafters of the farmhouse, over the top of which are seen angels looking down, while shafts of light from the sky on the left illuminate them.

Cleaned and repaired in 1936, and surface cleaned in 1948. In fairly good condition.

Derived from an identical composition: an altarpiece by Paolo Veronese in the Church of Santa Corona at Vicenza, painted for Marcantonio Cogoli about 1574. The follower or imitator who painted the painting at Wilton sought to heighten the

dramatic effect by turning it into a night scene, and it is about one third of the size of the Veronese altarpiece, which was copied many times by painters active in Vicenza in the seventeenth century.

Provenance: One of the eight pictures presented to Philip, 5th Earl of Pembroke, by the Grand-Duke Cosimo III in 1669, as by Veronese.

Italian School, XVII Century

230. ST MARY MAGDALEN
Canvas, $35\frac{1}{2} \times 27$ in.

Half length, naked to the waist, her long golden hair being held by her right hand across her breast, her left hand holding a robe below her waist. Her head is tilted back as she gazes upwards.

Much rubbed; cleaned and repaired in 1934.

A copy after the painting by Titian in the Pitti Palace in Florence; another version is in the Hermitage Gallery. In both these paintings, the face is much more masculine and harder.

Provenance: One of the eight pictures presented to Philip, 5th Earl of Pembroke, by the Grand-Duke Cosimo III in 1669 (see Introduction). The inscription on the back of the canvas by a later hand reads: 'Il dono dil Gran: Duca da Fior: a Filip Com di Pembr: Tiziano P.'
Wilkinson records that a line engraving from the Wilton picture was executed by Hendrik Danckerts (1630–1678) under which is the inscription: 'Titianus pinxit. Henr: Dankers Hagae; Quia dilexit multum, remissa ei multa peccata. Ex Collectis Comitis Pembrockiae.'

Italian School, XVII Century
Copy after Raphael

231. MADONNA AND CHILD
Wood, $12\frac{1}{2} \times 9$ in.

The Virgin is seated wearing a green and brown dress, looking down at the naked Christ, who is sitting on a white cushion on her lap, holding out towards her with both hands a lily. A green curtain is behind the Virgin's head, and an open window is above the Child. In gold on a red border to the top of the Virgin's dress are the words: 'Raphaelo Urbinas MDVIII.'

Cleaned in 1939.

This is perhaps a seventeenth-century version of Raphael's Madonna with the Rose, and is coarsely drawn and painted.

Provenance: At Wilton before 1730; probably bought by Thomas, 8th Earl of Pembroke. Gambarini (p. 94) calls it 'Raphael Urbino' and gives a description of it in seven lines, saying 'the flesh is so tenderly painted as if one might dent it with one's finger', which is far from true; he goes on to say 'it was grav'd by Morien'. Jean Morin died in 1666.

Literature: Passavant says it is completely repainted and Raphael had nothing to do with it.

Italian School, XVII Century, Copy after Andrea Solario (c. 1460–1515)

232. MADONNA AND CHILD

Wood, $16\frac{1}{4} \times 12$ in.

The Virgin in a red and blue dress and green skirt, looks down on the naked infant Christ, who lies on a cushion, and is about to be breast-fed. Background of rocks and trees in the centre, on either side of which are distant views of a river, villages, trees and hills.

Cleaned and repaired in 1935. In fair condition.

This is a very poor copy of the painting by Andrea Solario in the Museo Poldi-Pezzoli in Milan (No. 602). The composition of the Virgin and Child is the same, but the background is different. The drawing and painting of the Child and the Virgin's hands is so bad that over-painting is suspected, and X-ray examination might reveal something different, especially as the background is infinitely superior.

Provenance: At Wilton before 1730; probably bought by Thomas, 8th Earl of Pembroke. Gambarini (p. 31): 'Andrea Solari, the Virgin with Christ at her breast; the landskip over her shoulders shows little figures of persons and horses wonderful neat.'

Versions: Louvre, Paris, 'Virgin of the green pillow'; Carrara Academy, Bergamo.

Italian School, XVII Century

233. HEAD OF AN OLD MAN (ST PAUL?)

Canvas, 31×26 in.

Head and shoulders; the white-bearded head, covered by a black hood, is turned to the left, a strong light playing on the face. His right hand is across his breast.

Cleaned and repaired in 1934. Somewhat rubbed, otherwise in fairly good condition.

Provenance: Bought by Thomas, 8th Earl of Pembroke, before 1730. It is more than probable that this is the picture mentioned by Gambarini as *St Paul* by Gobbo de' Carracci: 'St Paul with a beard so freely painted that several painters have copied it in London'. The attribution by Gambarini may be correct. Pietro Paolo Bonzi was born in Cortona in the second half of the sixteenth century, and was known as Il Gobbo (the Hunchback). He was not a successful portrait painter, but became well known for his paintings of fruit. He died aged about 60.

Italian School, XVII Century

234. VENUS AT VULCAN'S FORGE

Wood, $8\frac{3}{4} \times 17$ in.

Venus, with a red ribbon in her hair and slightly draped in a blue robe, stands holding a cherub in her hand with the three naked Graces on the right. Vulcan stands, nearly naked, with a wooden leg, between the forge on the left, where a naked man is working the bellows, and the anvil, round which three other naked men are standing, all with hammers. Landscape background.

Cleaned in 1962. In fair condition.

Provenance: At Wilton before 1730, probably bought by Thomas, 8th Earl of Pembroke. Gambarini (p. 108) says it is by 'Alessandro Turco Veronese called also Orbetto'.

Italian School, First Half of the XVII Century

235. THE MARRIAGE OF ST CATHERINE

Canvas, 11×8 in.

The Virgin is seated, to the left, wearing a pink dress and a blue cloak, holding the naked Child, who is placing the ring on the left hand of St Catherine in a yellow dress and green cloak; she is seen kneeling on the right. Behind the Virgin stands Joseph, with St Elizabeth's head showing behind the Child. Architectural background.

Cleaned in 1933. In fair condition.

Provenance: Probably bought by Thomas, 8th Earl of Pembroke. Gambarini (p. 107) says it is signed and dated 1587, and Wilkinson mentions a signature 'Sofon. Anguisciola. f. MDLXXX . . .', but it is no longer visible, and in style and general treatment appears to be of the seventeenth century, and if not Italian, it could possibly be a Flemish copy.

Italian School, ? XVIII Century

236. DON GARCIA DE MEDICI

Canvas, 12½ × 9½ in.

Aged about two, with brown eyes and hair, with a round pink face, he wears a dark-blue coat with dashes of white like snow flakes or leaves, over a white shirt. A double gold chain, like an order, is worn over the shoulders and chest. His right hand, which holds a pear, rests on a table, and his left hand touches his chest.

Cleaned in 1955.

Don Garcia was the son of Cosimo I, Grand Duke of Tuscany, and Eleanor of Toledo.
The identity of the child was recognized by the late Duke of Alba.

Provenance: There is no trace of this painting in any of the eighteenth-century catalogues, so it may have been acquired some time in the nineteenth century, but it is a very poor copy of an original by Bronzino.

Italian School, XVIII Century

237. GENERAL PASCAL PAOLI WITH SOME OF HIS SOLDIERS

Canvas, 17¼ × 14 in.

Seated, with white hair; his head is turned to his left. He wears a blue tunic with white frilly shirt and stockings, with black boots. His left hand is across his chest and his right rests on his thigh. Two soldiers in brown, one holding a stave, stand on his left, and another bearded one in brown, holding a club, stands on his right, and he wears black goatskin trousers. A large brown dog is in the foreground, and a white coat of arms is painted in the background.

On the back of the frame is written 'Gen: di Paoli, some Corsican soldiers about him, and his dog Cosacco, the Arms of Corsica in the background'.

Pascal Paoli was born in 1725, son of Hyacinthe Paoli. He followed his father as leader of the Corsican revolutionaries in 1755 against the Genoese. He was defeated in 1769, and came to England, where he met Dr Johnson and Boswell, and Henry, 10th Earl of Pembroke, who later visited him in Corsica, to which he returned after the French Revolution. Subsequently he drove the French from the island, which was placed under British protection. He finally settled in England, where he died in 1807.

Provenance: Probably painted by an amateur in Corsica, and given to Henry, 10th Earl of Pembroke.

SPANISH SCHOOL

Jusepe Ribera ('Lo Spagnoletto')

1591–1652

Born at Xativa, near Valencia. Visited Rome, where he studied under Caravaggio; he worked for many years in Naples (where he died), returning to Spain at intervals under the patronage of Philip IV.

238. DEMOCRITUS   *Plate* 112

Canvas, 61 × 47 in.

Full length, seated, dressed in rags and barefooted, holding an open book. He is laughing at 'the follies of the world'.

Democritus (about 400 B.C.), the philosopher, was celebrated for his wit and gaiety.

Re-lined and cleaned in 1907, and cleaned in 1937. In very good condition.

Provenance: Gambarini records that it came from the collection of 'Cardinal de Medici', so that it was purchased either by Philip, the 4th Earl, or Thomas, the 8th Earl.

UNKNOWN SCHOOLS

Unknown, XVIII Century

239. LANDSCAPE

Canvas, $16 \times 20\frac{3}{4}$ in.

A solitary figure in a red cap, with his back turned, follows some sheep down a path in a wooded hill towards a distant plain and village.

Cleaned in 1961.

Provenance: Not known; probably acquired in the nineteenth century.

240. PORTRAIT OF A YOUNG MAN

Canvas on wood, $22\frac{1}{2} \times 17\frac{1}{2}$ in.

Head and shoulders; dark brown hair, brown eyes, full lips, the head turned slightly to his left. He wears a fur-trimmed red cloak, fastened across the front by a gold clasp, over a green uniform with gold lacing.

This unknown young officer, judging from his appearance and uniform, appears to be foreign, but whether Russian, which might be the case, or Italian, which is also probable, it is hard to say. The painting is certainly of the eighteenth century.

Provenance: There is no record of the acquisition of this painting, and it is not mentioned in any previous catalogue.

241. A WHITE HORSE

Wood, 9×12 in.

Facing to the right, the white horse with brown markings, has a mane and tail reaching to the ground.

Cleaned in 1960.

Provenance: Perhaps bought by or given to Henry, 10th Earl of Pembroke.

ADDENDUM TO THE DUTCH SCHOOL

By or after Jan van Goyen
1596-1656

Born at Leyden, and studied under a number of painters; after travelling through France, he returned to Holland, first to Haarlem, and then to Leyden. Later he went to The Hague, where he died.

242. RIVER SCENE WITH FERRY BOATS

Wood, $12 \times 19\frac{3}{4}$ in.

In the centre foreground is a ferry boat, in which is a man on a horse, two men, two women, a child and a dog. The boat is being pushed off the bank by another man, behind whom is another figure with a dog. Behind him is a small building, outside which a group of people are standing, with two more figures and some cattle on a high bank in front of some trees. A man is rowing a woman across the water in a small boat just in front of the ferry boat, and two men are taking three cows across the river in another boat. Behind them on the far bank can be seen a village.

Cleaned in 1934. In very good condition.

Provenance: At Wilton before 1730; Gambarini, p. 65, attributes it to Herman Saftleven (1609-1685), who was a pupil of Van Goyen. This may be correct, and it is to be noted that this painting is not signed, as most of Van Goyen's paintings are.

THE CEILINGS AND MURALS

Ceiling in the Little Ante-room

Lorenzo Sabbatini

1530–1577

Born in Bologna, where he worked as well as in Rome.

THE BIRTH OF VENUS

Canvas, $57\frac{1}{2} \times 74$ in.

Venus is rising from a shell in the sea; close by are two Tritons, and the three Graces are seated on the shore to her left, one with flowers, another with a scarf, while three winged cherubs, one in a chariot, are in the foreground, and two more in the clouds above Venus.

This painting, which is rather in the style of Primaticcio, and is poorly drawn and painted, was badly damaged by water when the bathroom above overflowed in 1952; it was re-lined and cleaned and repaired that same year.

Provenance: At Wilton before 1730; Gambarini (p. 15) attributes it to Lorenzino da Bologna, and its position then in 1731, was 'In the Cube painted room', therefore hanging on the wall. By 1751, Cowdry says it was 'in the Closet' (now called the little ante-room) in the Ceiling.

Bought by Thomas, 8th Earl of Pembroke.

Ceiling in the Corner Room

Luca Giordano

1632–1705

Born in Naples, the son of a painter, he studied under Ribera. After travelling to Rome, he came under the notice of Pietro da Cortona, for whom he worked for some time, before achieving recognition on his own. He worked thereafter in Venice, Naples and Florence, before finally going to Spain as Court Painter to Charles II and Philip V. He died in Naples.

THE CONVERSION OF ST PAUL

Canvas, $88\frac{1}{2} \times 96$ in.

St Paul in armour, surrounded by six or seven other men in armour with their horses, falls backwards with his horse, dazzled by the blaze of light shooting from the clouds above them.

Provenance: Acquired before 1730; Gambarini (p. 36) records the painting correctly, but says it was 'on the Stair-case by the Great Hall' (destroyed by James Wyatt at the beginning of the nineteenth century). However, by 1751, the date of the next catalogue by Richard Cowdry, it was in its present position, as he says (p. 77) 'In the ceiling, the Conversion of St. Paul . . .' It was therefore placed there by Henry, 9th Earl of Pembroke, shortly before 1739, the last year in which Andien de Clermont (see below) was working at Wilton. Clermont's decoration of the plaster portion of the ceiling surrounding this canvas consists of trophies with Roman emblems, S.P.Q.R. swags, palm leaves, branches, and in the corners and over the chimney-piece, masks of men, encircled by wreaths, all painted in delicate colours of blue, red, grey, brown, green and bronze.

Ceiling in the Colonnade Room

Andien de Clermont

Died 1783

He came to England about 1716–17, perhaps as an assistant to Antoine Monnoyer, son of Baptiste Monnoyer, and proceeded to develop from a flower painter into a decorative artist, becoming an exponent of the 'Singerie' and grotesque form, and was employed in country houses on ceilings and murals. He worked for forty years in England before returning to France in 1756.

Henry, 9th Earl of Pembroke, known as the Architect Earl, employed Clermont to paint in whole or in part four ceilings in the State Rooms, and the Household Account Book of 1733–50 records the following entries:

Aug. 26. 1735.
    To the little French Painter on acct. £10. 10. 0.

Sep. 20. 1735.
    To the little French Painter on acct. £10. 10. 0.

Sep. 29. 1735.
    To the little French Painter on acct. £10. 10. 0.

Sep. 29. 1735.
    To the little French Painter on acct. £20. 10. 0.

Nov. 4. 1735.
    To the little French Painter Clermt. in full
                    £32. 10. 0.

Nov. 17. 1739.
    To Clermont for painting Ceilings at Wilton.
                  £130. 00. 0.

Oil on plaster.

Monkeys, birds, figures, flowers, cages, parasols, wreaths, coats of arms and ciphers are painted freely and lightly in bright colours. The 'Masks' of lions in 'Bronze' are painted in the corners.   *Plate 148*

Other houses which Clermont decorated, some of which still survive, were Narford Hall, Norfolk; Kirtlington Park, Oxford; a fishing pavilion for the 3rd Duke of Marlborough on Monkey Island at Bray; Radnor House, Twickenham (destroyed in World War II by bombs); and the dining-room at Strawberry Hill for Horace Walpole. A room at Wentworth Woodhouse may also be by him.

Ceiling in the Great Ante-room

Andien de Clermont

Oil on plaster.

Light clouds in a pale blue sky which is surrounded by green trellis-work and festoons of roses, broken by green coats of arms on four sides; in the rounded corners of the ceiling are 'Masks' of grotesque men, and also in the small squares at intervals in the trellis-work.

Ceiling in the Double-cube Room

Emanuel de Critz

1605–1665

Son of John de Critz, Serjeant Painter to James I and Charles I. Trained under his father; portrait and scene painter. Recorded as having executed 'sondry painted workes' of an unspecified nature at Whitehall and Westminster (*Decorative painting in England*, Vol. 1. Edward Croft-Murray). He was presumably recommended to Philip, 4th Earl of Pembroke, by Inigo Jones and John Webb.

THE STORY OF PERSEUS

Canvas.

The centre panel shows Perseus rescuing his mother from Polydectes; the flanking panels show Perseus and Andromeda, and Perseus and Pegasus. The colouring is exceptionally strong, and the figures are coarsely painted.

Edward Pierce

Pierce flourished in the reign of Charles I, who employed him in London mainly as a scene-painter under Inigo Jones. He died in 1658.

Coved ceiling; oil on plaster.

Swags of enormous fruit and vegetables held up by gigantic putti, as well as large urns and satyrs, the coat of arms in the centre of each end, the motto 'Ung Je Serviray' in the centre of each side, and the coronet above the P.M. in each corner, all painted in grey, on a brown background, occupy the entire length and breadth of the ceiling, sixty feet long and thirty feet wide together with the De Critz story of Perseus panels in the centre.

As Mr Croft-Murray says, the scale is somewhat overpowering, and the execution coarse, yet there is a theatrical effectiveness about it. Pierce must have finished this work by 1654 after Webb had completed the decoration, as Evelyn saw the room this year.

Ceiling and Murals in the Single Cube Room

Giuseppe Cesari
1568–1640

Born and died in Rome. Examples of his work of very mediocre quality, can be seen in some of the Galleries in Italy, France and Germany.

DAEDALUS AND ICARUS

Canvas, 132×120 in. In the centre of the ceiling.

The naked Icarus, a red cloak trailing below his feet, with burnt wings, falls headlong towards his naked father Daedalus, whose enormous wings stretch from one side of the canvas to the other, and who looks up in horror at his son.

Provenance: Gambarini (p. 7) says that this painting 'was brought out of a villa near Florence by the first Sir Charles Cotterell, for Earl Philip', meaning Philip, 4th Earl of Pembroke, so that it was obviously intended to form part of the ceiling decoration when the room was designed by Inigo Jones and John Webb and finished in 1653.

Matthew Gooderick
working 1616–1654

Gooderick was employed to decorate, in oil, the coved plaster portion of the ceiling, with grotesque designs in the late Renaissance manner in a variety of colours on a cream ground; the arms and motto of the Pembroke family are in the centre of each side. This decoration by Gooderick, whose last work this probably was, is in the same manner as the ceiling he painted for the Queen's bedroom of the Queen's House at Greenwich, but on a very much larger scale. Mr Croft-Murray thinks that Clermont may have restored or added to it just over eighty years later; cf. Edward Croft-Murray, *Decorative Painting in England*, Vol. 1, 1962.

Emanuel de Critz
1605–1665

Oil on wood. Twenty-six paintings of various sizes, on the panelling of the room, below the dado rail,

depicting scenes from Sir Philip Sidney's 'Arcadia'.

Painted at the same time as he was decorating the Double Cube ceiling with the story of Perseus. Both rooms were finished by 1654, when Evelyn visited Wilton on July 20, and records the work as by 'De Creete'. Aubrey calls him 'Emanuel De Cretz'. Gambarini (p. 6) says the Double Cube ceiling was by 'Signior Tommaso, a disciple of Caracci', and the Single Cube as by 'the brother of Signior Tommaso, who us'd to paint only small figures'. The other De Critz brother was called Thomas, who may have helped Emanuel. Lord Pembroke had already employed Emanuel to decorate a room or rooms in a house at The Cockpit, Whitehall, designed by Webb, as early as 1642.

Ceiling and Murals in the Hunting Room

Andien de Clermont

Oil on plaster, 30×20 ft.

A pale blue sky with light clouds, painted in an oval, surrounded by a broad dark-green border of garlands in a brown frieze linked to a broader 'architectural' frieze of brown, interspersed with rosettes and ribbons.

In this room, which is at the western end of the south front of the house, and may have been used as a dining-room, EDWARD PIERCE painted, about 1650–52, in oil, direct onto the panelling of the room, eighteen panels of hunting-scenes, European, Asiatic and African, after etchings by Antonio Tempesta in 'Il primo. libro di chacci di uccelli (1598), *Venationes Ferarum, Avium, Piscium* (1602)', and a series, without title, dedicated to Charles, Duc de Valois (1624). Philip, the 4th Earl of Pembroke, is shown on a white horse in one panel, and his son, Philip, the 5th Earl, is also shown on a white horse in the panel immediately below.   *Plates 142–147*

In between the hunting panels are long paintings of trophies in dark-green, perhaps by another hand, possibly Clermont.

The hunting panel measurements are as follows: eight of 69×36 in.; eight of 39×36 in.; one of 36×58 in.; and one of 38×45 in.

THE DRAWINGS

Italian (?), XVII Century

1. APOLLO AND MARSYAS   *Plate* 103

Standing together, Apollo seen from the back and looking to the right.

Red chalk, 15½ × 9 in. (Old mount, 17¾ × 11⅛ in.)

Provenance: Probably bought by Thomas, 8th Earl of Pembroke.

Dutch, Late XVII Century

2. A RIVERSIDE VILLAGE, WITH BOATS MOORED BESIDE A QUAY

Black chalk, 4⅜ × 7½ in.

Provenance: Presented by Mr Roger Senhouse to Sidney, 16th Earl of Pembroke, in 1936 on his marriage.

Dutch, XVIII Century

3. A VILLAGE SCENE, WITH A CHURCH AND TAVERN

Pen and brown ink, with grey wash, 6½ × 8 in.

4. A VILLAGE SCENE, WITH A CHURCH AND TAVERN

Pen and brown ink, with grey wash, 6⅜ × 8⅛ in.

Provenance: Presented by Jonkheer and Madame van Swinderen to Sidney, 16th Earl of Pembroke, in 1936 on his marriage.

Attributed to Bartholomeus van Bassen
Active from 1613, died 1652

5. HEAD OF AN INFANT

Red chalk, 5 × 3⅞ in.

Inscription: Recto, at the foot, *Bartolemeo Bassente.*

There is apparently no record of any artist who can be identified with 'Bartolemeo Bassente' except possibly the Dutch painter of interior perspectives, Bartholomeus van Bassen, working at Delft, The Hague, and in England between 1613 and 1650. No drawings, however, by Van Bassen are known;

and, moreover, it should be noted that the present inscription distinctly suggests an Italian provenance, and the artist in question is not recorded as having visited Italy.

Provenance: Presented by Lady Algernon Gordon-Lennox to Sidney, 16th Earl of Pembroke, in 1936 on his marriage.

Rosalba Carriera
1675–1757

Born in Venice, the daughter of Angelo Carriera, she studied under a number of minor painters, and was mainly influenced by Pietro Liberi. She quickly became a popular painter, first in oils, then in watercolours and crayons, and was elected a member of the Academies in Rome, Bologna and Florence. She visited Paris, where she received many commissions, and later Vienna and Modena, returning to Venice, where she became blind ten years before her death.

6. A CUPID SEEN FROM BEHIND, HOLDING A BOW IN HIS RIGHT HAND, AND LYING ON CLOUDS
                                          Plate 107

Black and red chalk, heightened with white, 15 × 10¾ in. (Old mount, 15⅛ × 11⅛ in.)

Inscription: Recto, in lower left hand corner, *Rosalba.*

Provenance: Probably bought by Thomas, 8th Earl of Pembroke.

Sebastiano Conca
1679–1764

Born at Gaëta, and studied under Francesco Solimena. He worked in Rome, painting portraits and frescoes, and also travelled in Italy, Germany, Spain and Poland. He died in Naples.

7. NESSUS AND DEJANIRA

Pen and ink, with brown wash, heightened with yellow body colour on purple-brown paper, 12⅛ × 8⅛ in.

Inscription: Recto, in lower right hand corner, *Seb: Concha.*

Provenance: Probably bought by Thomas, 8th Earl of Pembroke. Sold with other drawings by Old Masters, on July 9, 1917, lot No. 322, for £4. 15. 0. (Sotheby's). Purchased by a group of friends nineteen years later and presented by them to Sidney, 16th Earl of Pembroke, on his marriage in July 1936.

By or after Correggio
1494–1534

Correggio, the son of Pellegrino Allegri, a tradesman, was born in Correggio; his early training is not known with any certainty, but he studied in Modena and Mantua, and was greatly influenced by the works of Mantegna. He settled in Parma, where he painted the great dome of the cathedral, and numerous religious pictures. He returned to Correggio in 1530, where he died at the age of 40.

8. HEAD OF A PUTTO, TURNED TO THE LEFT, AND LOOKING OVER HIS LEFT SHOULDER   *Plate* 89

Black chalk, heightened with white, on grey paper, the corners cut off, $17\frac{3}{4} \times 15$ in. (Old mount, $19 \times 16\frac{1}{4}$ in.)

Provenance: Probably bought by Thomas, 8th Earl of Pembroke.

This and No. 9 are studies either for or after the destroyed fresco in the apse of S. Giovanni Evangelista, Parma (cf. the copy by Annibale Carracci in the Gallery at Parma. *K. der K.* 56 and 57).

9. HEAD OF AN ANGEL, LOOKING OVER HIS LEFT SHOULDER

Black and coloured chalks, $19\frac{1}{2} \times 14\frac{3}{8}$ in. (Old mount, $20\frac{1}{2} \times 15\frac{1}{2}$ in.)

Inscription: Recto, on the old mount in the centre, *Cor:*

Provenance: As No. 8.

Antoine Coypel
1661–1722

Born in Paris, the son of Noel Coypel, also a painter, who took him to Rome, aged eleven, to study; he returned to Paris when he was eighteen, and two years later became a member of the French Academy. He received commissions for cathedrals, churches and some of the royal palaces, and by 1716 he had been appointed principal painter to the King. He died in Paris.

10. A YOUNG ZEPHYR PLAYING A PIPE   *Plate* 117

Half length in profile to the right, with drapery about his loins.

Red and black chalks, heightened with white, on brown-toned paper, $11\frac{7}{8} \times 9\frac{7}{8}$ in.

Provenance: Probably bought by Thomas, 8th Earl of Pembroke.

Attributed to Coypel

11. HEAD OF A WOMAN IN A TURBAN, TO THE FRONT AND LOOKING DOWN   *Plate* 118

Black and red chalks, heightened with white, on brown-toned paper, 9×10 in.

Provenance: As No. 10.

Carlo Dolci
1616–1686

Born at Florence, where he worked all his life.

12. AN APOSTLE (?)   *Plate* 104

Full length, turned half left, and looking downwards. Wearing a red gown with a cloak over it.

Black and red chalks, touched with white, on blue-gray paper, $16\frac{5}{8} \times 10\frac{3}{8}$ in. (Old mount, $17\frac{3}{8} \times 12\frac{3}{8}$ in.)

Inscription: Recto, in the lower left hand corner, *di Carlin Dolci;* and on a slip of paper attached to the old mount, in the upper left hand corner, *Carlo Dolce & 2 of his Chief Disciples.*

Provenance: Probably bought by Thomas, 8th Earl of Pembroke.

13. BUST OF ST JOHN THE DIVINE, LOOKING TO FRONT, WITH HIS HEAD BENT OVER HIS RIGHT SHOULDER   *Plate* 105

Black and red chalks, $11\frac{7}{8} \times 8\frac{1}{2}$ in. (Old mount, 15×11 in.)

Inscription: Recto, in the lower left hand corner, *L.CAR:PI:;* and the lower right hand corner

ST. I: APOS:; and on the old mount, at the foot, *Ludovico Caraccii. Bologna* 1555–1619.

Provenance: As No. 12.

The attribution to Carlo Dolci has been suggested by Mr Philip Pouncey and Mr John Gere.

Gabriel François Doyen
1726–1806

Born in Paris; studied under Van Loo, winning the Grand Prix de Rome in 1746. He became a member of the French Academy in 1759, and Professor in 1776. He decorated the chapel of St Gregoire in the Invalides, and in 1791 went to Russia, where he worked for Catherine II and Paul I and was appointed Director of the Academy at St Petersburg, where he died.

14. SCENE FROM ROMAN HISTORY(?)
Pen and ink, with brown wash, heightened with white, over black chalk, $19 \times 24\frac{1}{2}$ in.

Provenance: Probably bought by Henry, 10th Earl, or George, 11th Earl of Pembroke.

William Hoare
1706–1792

Born at Eye in Suffolk; studied for eight or nine years in Italy, and on his return settled in Bath, where he worked mainly in pastels and crayons. He was one of the foundation members of the Royal Academy.

15. HENRY, 9TH EARL OF PEMBROKE (1693–1750)
Plate 129
Bust, with head turned slightly to the right, wearing a powdered wig.
Red and black chalk, heightened with white, on brown paper, $12\frac{1}{4} \times 10\frac{7}{8}$ in.

Provenance: Commissioned by the 9th Earl in 1744.

16. MARY FITZWILLIAM, COUNTESS OF PEMBROKE, WIFE OF THE ABOVE
Plate 130
Bust, in profile to the right, wearing a muslin cap on her powdered hair, and a triple row pearl necklace.

Red and black chalk, heightened with white, on brown paper, $12\frac{1}{4} \times 11\frac{3}{8}$ in.

Provenance: As No. 15.

17. HENRY, LORD HERBERT, THEIR SON
Plate 131
Bust, in profile to the right, wearing a black velvet riding cap on his powdered hair.
Black and red chalk, heightened with white, on brown paper, $12 \times 11\frac{1}{2}$ in.

Provenance: As No. 15.

Hans Holbein, the Younger
1497/8–1543

For his life, see No. 191 above.

18. SIR GEORGE NEVILL, 5TH LORD ABERGAVENNY (? 1460–1535)
Plate 41
Black and coloured chalks, touched with white, on pink prepared paper, $10\frac{3}{4} \times 9\frac{1}{4}$ in. (Old mount $14\frac{1}{4} \times 12$ in.)

Inscription: In the lower left hand corner, *LORD CROMWELL.* And in the lower right hand corner, *HOLBEIN.*

Bust, turned half right; wearing a black cap, and a furred gown.

Son of the 4th Lord Abergavenny, he was created a Knight of the Bath by Richard III, fought for Henry VIII in France, and became Constable of Dover Castle and Lord Warden of the Cinque Ports.

Provenance: One of the set of famous men and women at the Court of Henry VIII, drawn for the King, about 1530. Charles I exchanged this book of drawings with William, 3rd Earl of Pembroke, for the *St. George*, by Raphael, now in the National Gallery, Washington (see K. T. Parker, *The Drawings of Hans Holbein . . . at Windsor Castle*, Phaidon Press, 1945, pp. 1–20). The main series of the drawings seems to have returned to the Royal Collection by 1675 (see Parker, p. 16), but the present study of Lord Abergavenny was retained by the Pembroke family presumably because the sitter had been a friend and contemporary of William, 1st Earl of Pembroke. This and the study of Anne Boleyn, formerly in the collection of Jonathan Richardson I, and now in that of the Earl of Bradford at Weston, are the only two outside the series at Windsor Castle.

Exhibited: Tudor Exhibition, 1890 (No. 1414); Burlington Fine Arts Club, 1909 (No. 70); Works by Holbein and other Masters of the sixteenth and seventeenth centuries, Royal Academy, London, 1950–51 (No. 90); Art Treasures of the West Country, Bristol, 1937 (No. 182).

Literature: Vasari Society V, 28; Ganz, *Les Dessins de Hans Holbein le jeune*, 1911/26, I, 37 (*Catalogue raisonné*, 1939, No. 37).

Benedetto Luti

1666–1724

Born in Florence, he was a pupil of Antonio Gabbiani; after travelling to Rome under the patronage of the Grand Duke Cosimo III, he received commissions including those from Pope Clement XI, which earned him papal decorations, but he preferred drawing to painting.

19. HEAD AND SHOULDERS OF A YOUNG WOMAN, TURNED TO THE RIGHT, AND LOOKING BACK OVER HER RIGHT SHOULDER   *Plate* 106

Black chalk on grey paper, $14\frac{1}{2}\times 9\frac{7}{8}$ in. (Old mount, $16\frac{3}{4}\times 12\frac{3}{8}$ in.)

Inscription: Recto, in the lower left hand corner, *Cav: Benedetto Lutti.*

Provenance: Probably bought by Thomas, 8th Earl of Pembroke.

Giovanni Battista Piazzetta

1682–1754

Born at Venice. He was a pupil of Antonio Molinari, later going to Bologna, where he was influenced by Crespi and Guercino. He was back in Venice by 1711, where he worked for various churches and painted portraits, as well as doing illustrations for books, and numerous drawings. In 1750 he was elected Director of the Venetian Academy and died in Venice four years later.

20. A YOUTH ENJOINING A MAIDEN TO SILENCE
Black chalk, heightened with white, on grey paper, $15\frac{1}{8}\times 12$ in.

21. BUST OF A WOMAN, WITH HER LEFT HAND TO HER BREAST
Black chalk, heightened with white, on grey paper, $15\frac{1}{8}\times 12$ in.

22. BUST OF A YOUNG WOMAN, LEANING ON HER RIGHT HAND
Black chalk, heightened with white, on grey paper, $15\frac{1}{4}\times 12\frac{1}{4}$ in.

Perhaps a portrait of Giulia Lama as a young woman.

23. BUST OF A YOUTH AND A YOUNG WOMAN, HE LOOKING AT HER OVER HIS RIGHT SHOULDER
Black chalk, heightened with white on grey paper, $15\frac{1}{4}\times 12$ in.

24. BUST OF A BEARDED OLD MAN WEARING A SKULL CAP AND FUR-TRIMMED GOWN, AND HOLDING UP A PAPER
Black chalk, heightened with white, on grey paper, $15\frac{1}{4}\times 12\frac{1}{8}$ in.

25. BUST OF AN APOSTLE (?) LOOKING TO THE FRONT AND RESTING HIS HEAD ON HIS LEFT HAND
Black chalk, heightened with white, on grey paper, $15\frac{1}{4}\times 12\frac{1}{8}$ in.

Provenance: Probably bought by Thomas, 8th Earl of Pembroke (d. 1733), or Henry, 9th Earl (d. 1750).

Raphael

1483–1520

Born in Urbino, son of the painter Giovanni Santi. In 1504 he worked in Florence, where he came under the influence of Leonardo da Vinci. Later he was employed by the Popes to decorate rooms in the Vatican. In 1514 he was appointed architect of St Peter's. He died in Rome.

26. HEAD OF A CARDINAL, TURNED HALF RIGHT, WEARING A RED BIRETTA   *Plate* 87
Black chalk, with red and white chalk smudged together to make pink on the face; the cap in red chalk only, $11\frac{7}{8}\times 9\frac{3}{8}$ in.

Inscription: Recto, in gold letters in lower left hand corner on the old mount, *R.URB: PI:* and in the lower right hand corner on the old mount, *P. LEO X.*

In the lower right hand corner of the drawing itself is the Lely stamp in black *PL.*

Verso, in a seventeenth-century hand on a strip of paper, pasted onto the brown paper protecting the back: *Ritratto del Cardinale Giulio de' Medici, fatto dal vivo, per mettere nel Quadro di Leon Decimo, che sta nelle stanze del Gran Duca di Fiorenza, dentro al quale quadro è il ritratto del istesso Papa, con quegli del sopra detto Cardinale, et il Cardinale de' Rossi, fatto della mano propria di Raffaello d'Urbino.*

Provenance: Sir Peter Lely (*Lugt* 2092); Thomas, 8th Earl of Pembroke.

The attribution to Raphael dates from the time of Lely, and has been confirmed by the Department of Prints and Drawings at the British Museum, who point out that the use of colour is most unusual.

The subject of the drawing has not been identified, but is probably a Cardinal at the Court of Pope Leo X, to whom there is some resemblance, though it is not thought to be the Pope himself.

In 1966 Professor Konrad Oberhuber saw the drawing at Wilton and said that it can only be by Raphael himself.

After Raphael

27. HEADS OF RAPHAEL AND SODOMA, FROM 'THE PHILOSOPHY' (THE SCHOOL OF ATHENS) FRESCO, STANZA DELLA SEGNATURA, IN THE VATICAN

Red and black chalks, 16×12 in. (Old mount $17\frac{1}{4} \times 13\frac{1}{4}$ in.)

Inscription: Recto, on the old mount, *R.Urbin & his Master Perugino, in Sc: Ath.*

Provenance: Probably bought by Thomas, 8th Earl of Pembroke.

28. HEAD OF BRAMANTE (?) FROM 'THE THEOLOGY' (LA DISPUTA DEL SACRAMENTO), FRESCO, STANZA DELLA SEGNATURA, IN THE VATICAN

Red and black chalks, $16 \times 12\frac{1}{4}$ in. (Old mount, $17 \times 13\frac{1}{4}$ in.)

Inscription: Recto, on the old mount, *Bramante in Div: Sc:*

Provenance: As No. 27.

Sir Joshua Reynolds, P.R.A.
1723–1792

29. HENRY, 9TH EARL OF PEMBROKE, AND HIS WIFE

Red chalk. Perhaps originally on two separate leaves of a sketch-book, each $7\frac{3}{8} \times 6$ in. They are mounted on a large sheet of paper to form a double portrait within an oval, the overall measurements being $12\frac{1}{2} \times 16\frac{1}{2}$ in.

Half length, seated opposite each other, he reading, she sewing.

Provenance: As the 9th Earl died in 1749–50, Reynolds must have made this sketch in London just after his return from Italy in the last year of Lord Pembroke's life.

On one of the Reynolds receipts at Wilton is the entry 'for a drawing of the late Lord. £2. 2. 0.'.

The date is 1763, on a receipt for paintings, so that it seems probable that Reynolds told the 10th Earl that he had done these sketches fourteen years before, and that if he would like them, he would take them out of the sketch book, mount them on a larger sheet, and finish it off.

E. Easton in *A new description of Wilton,* 7th Edn., 1776, p. 64, refers to a drawing by Reynolds of 'The late Lord and Lady Pembroke'.

Mr Oliver Millar noticed this sketch, which is framed, on one of his visits to Wilton in 1965, and identified the sitters and the artist.

After Giulio Romano
1492–1546

Romano was born Giulio dei Giannuzzi in Rome, and was apprenticed to Raphael, becoming one of his best pupils. His most famous works are the frescoes in the Palazzo del Tè in Mantua, which he also designed.

30. HEAD OF JUSTICE, IN PROFILE TO THE RIGHT   *Plate* 90

Red chalk, $14\frac{3}{8} \times 10\frac{1}{8}$ in. (Old mount, $16\frac{1}{8} \times 11\frac{3}{4}$ in.)

Inscription: Recto, on old mount, in lower left hand corner, *Justice in Constantine's Hall.*

Provenance: Probably bought by Thomas, 8th Earl of Pembroke.

Sir Peter Paul Rubens after Federigo Barocci

31. THE MARTYRDOM OF S. VITALIS   *Plate 47*

Pen and brown ink, with colour washes of rose, grey, green, and yellow ochre, heightened with red chalk and white body-colour. 20⅛ × 14⅛ in.

Inscription: Recto, in the centre at the foot, in ink, by Rubens, *federige Barocci dUrbino*.

The drawing has hitherto been described as by Barocci because of the inscription, but in 1964 Mr Michael Jaffé, after being told about the drawing a few months earlier by Dr Sherman Lee, examined it carefully, coming to the conclusion that it was wholly by Rubens after the famous altar-piece (now in Milan) painted by Barocci for the High Altar of the Church of S. Vitale at Ravenna. Mr A. E. Popham saw the drawing in 1935 and recognized it as by one hand, either by Rubens or one of his school.

Barocci was one of Rubens's favourite painters; Rubens made slight changes from the original painting, to suit his purpose, and has inscribed Barocci's name in order to remind his pupils that the altar-piece was painted by Barocci.

Provenance: Philip Lankrink (*Lugt*, No. 2090). Thomas, 8th Earl of Pembroke.

Literature: 'Rubens as a collector of drawings', part two (Michael Jaffé, *Master Drawings*, Master Drawings Association Inc., New York, Volume 3, No. 1, 1965), No. 27 in text, plate 22.

Luca Signorelli (?)

C. 1441–1523

Born at Cortona; he was a pupil of Piero della Francesca, and was also influenced by Antonio Pollaiuolo. He painted frescoes in Orvieto, Florence, Rome and Cortona, as well as many altarpieces.

32. ST JOHN THE DIVINE WRITING   *Plate 80*

Red chalk, touched with white. 16¼ × 10½ in. (Old mount, 17¼ × 11⅜ in.)

Inscription: Recto, in the lower left hand corner,

S.Di:, and on the old mount in the lower left hand corner, *IM.DIV:SCH:*.

Provenance: Probably bought by Thomas, 8th Earl of Pembroke.

Francesco Solimena

1657–1747

Born near Naples at Nocera de Pagani, son of a painter, under whom he was taught. He worked in Naples under Giacomo del Pò, and later worked in Rome and Assisi. He died in Naples.

33. THE NATIVITY   *Plate 108*

Brush drawing in brown wash over black chalk, heightened with white (oxidised). 16⅛ × 9¾ in. (Old mount, 17½ × 11¼ in.)

Inscription: Recto, on the old mount, at the foot in the centre, *Solimena*, and in the lower right hand corner, *P.L.*

Verso, in an eighteenth-century hand, *Roma & Arezzo*.

Fran^co Solimena Neapolitano impara da suo Padre e dal vedere l'opera di Luca Giordano si rende celebre, naque pittore, che con poca scola ameta oggi Gia molto grido, che siamo del 1698. ed il 42. di sua eta. Questo dissegno la mandò in Roma al Pre Sebastiano Resta, dal que l'ebbi io fr. Pellegrino Ant: o Orlandi Carmelitano da Bologna dilettante di desegni e pittura.

Provenance: Probably bought by Thomas, 8th Earl of Pembroke.

Attributed to Antonio Tempesta

1555–1630

34A. *Recto:* A KNIGHT IN ARMOUR WITH A TILTING SPEAR, ON A REARING HORSE   *Plate 95*

Pen and brown ink with brown wash, 12¼ × 10 in.

34B. *Verso:* ORPHEUS, SEATED, PLAYING A 'LIRA DA BRACCIO', AND A MAIDEN DANCING *Plate 96*

Pen and brown ink, with washes of brown and purple, over black chalk.

Provenance: Presented by the 7th Duke of Wellington to Sidney, 16th Earl of Pembroke, in 1936 on his marriage.

Gerard Ter Borch
1617–1681

Born at Zwolle, he studied under his father. He worked at Haarlem, in England, Italy, Germany, Spain, France, and in Holland in Amsterdam, Zwolle and Deventer, where he died.

35. A YOUNG MAN, SEATED ASTRIDE A ROCK OR BLOCK OF STONE, HIS LEFT ARM OUTSTRETCHED, WEARING A BROAD-BRIMMED HAT, DOUBLET AND BREECHES   *Plate* 74

Brush drawing in grey wash, touched with white over black chalk, on grey prepared paper, $8\frac{1}{2} \times 6\frac{5}{8}$ in.

Provenance: Presented by Sir Kenneth Clark to Sidney, 16th Earl of Pembroke, in 1935.

Antoine Watteau
1684–1721

Born at Valenciennes, the son of a plumber, he worked in Paris under Gillot and Audran. It was some years before his work was appreciated; he visited England two years before his death.

36. A COUNTRY BOY, STANDING TO FRONT, WITH CROSSED ARMS AND LEGS APART, AND WEARING A THREE-CORNERED HAT   *Plate* 120

Black and red chalk, $7\frac{1}{8} \times 3\frac{7}{8}$ in.

Provenance: Presented by Sir Kenneth Clark to Sidney, 16th Earl of Pembroke, in 1936 on his marriage.

PLATES

1. School of Hans Eworth: *Sir William Herbert, 1st Earl of Pembroke, K.G.* (Cat. No. 146)

2. Sir Anthony van Dyck: *William, 3rd Earl of Pembroke, K.G.* (Cat. No. 159)

3. Daniel Mytens: *Philip, 4th Earl of Pembroke and 1st Earl of Montgomery, K.G.* (Cat. No. 118)

4. Sir Anthony van Dyck: *Philip, 4th Earl of Pembroke, with his second wife, Anne Clifford, his daughter Sophia and her husband Robert, Earl of Carnarvon* (Detail of Cat. No. 158)

5. Sir Peter Lely: *The Hon. James Herbert and his wife Jane Spiller* (Cat. No. 42)

6. Sir Anthony van Dyck: *Charles, Lord Herbert, his wife, Mary Villiers, and his brother Philip, later 5th Earl of Pembroke*
(Detail of Cat. No. 158)

7. Sir Anthony van Dyck: *Philip, 5th Earl of Pembroke*
(Cat. No. 161)

8. Sir Peter Lely: *Catherine Villiers,
Countess of Pembroke* (Cat. No. 44)

9. Sir Peter Lely: *William, 6th Earl of Pembroke*
(Cat. No. 43)

10. Sir Peter Lely: *Henriette de Kerouaille,
Countess of Pembroke* (Cat. No. 41)

11. Willem Wissing:
Thomas, 8th Earl of Pembroke, K.G.
(Cat. No. 134)

12. Jan van der Vaart:
Margaret Sawyer, Countess of Pembroke
(Cat. No. 129)

13. Michael Dahl: *Barbara, Countess of Pembroke*
(Cat. No. 16)

14. Jonathan Richardson: *Lady Catherine Herbert and
the Hon. Robert Herbert* (Cat. No. 74)

15. Jonathan Richardson: *Henry, Lord Herbert, afterwards 9th Earl of Pembroke* (Cat. No. 73)

16. Pompeo Batoni: *Henry, 10th Earl of Pembroke* (Cat. No. 198)

17. David Morier: *Henry, 10th Earl of Pembroke* (Cat. No. 47)

18. Sir Joshua Reynolds: *Henry, 10th Earl of Pembroke, and his son George, Lord Herbert* (Cat. No. 63)

19. Sir Joshua Reynolds: *Elizabeth, Countess of Pembroke* (Cat. No. 64)

20. George Lambert: *View of Westcombe House, Blackheath* (Cat. No. 34)

21. George Lambert: *View of Westcombe House, Blackheath* (Cat. No. 36)

22. Richard Wilson: *Wilton House from the South East* (Cat. No. 83)

23. Richard Wilson: *Wilton House, South View from the Garden* (Cat. No. 85)

24. Sir Joshua Reynolds: *Henry, 10th Earl of Pembroke* (Cat. No. 65)

25. Sir Joshua Reynolds: *Elizabeth, Countess of Pembroke, and her son George, Lord Herbert* (Cat. No. 66)

26. Pompeo Batoni: *George, Lord Herbert* (Cat. No. 199)   27. Prince Hoare: *Lady Charlotte Herbert* (Cat. No. 22)

28. Sir William Beechey: *Lady Herbert* (Cat. No. 7)

29. Sir William Beechey:
Captain Augustus Montgomery (Cat. No. 8)

30. Sir Francis Grant: *Catherine, Countess of Pembroke* (Detail of Cat. No. 20)

31. Sir Francis Grant: *Sidney, Lord Herbert of Lea* (Detail of Cat. No. 19)

32. Hugo van der Goes: *The Adoration of the Shepherds* (Cat. No. 149)

33. Flemish School, XVI or early XVII Century: *The Devil tempting Christ to turn Stone into Bread* (Cat. No. 177)

34. Jan Gossaert: *The Children of Christian II, King of Denmark* (Cat. No. 150)

35. School of Bernard van Orley: *The Virgin and Child with St Anne and an Angel* (Cat. No. 153)

36. South German School: *The Entombment* (Cat. No. 194)

37. Lucas van Leyden: *The Card Players* (Cat. No. 116)

38. Lucas van Leyden: *The Card Players* (Detail of Cat. No. 116)

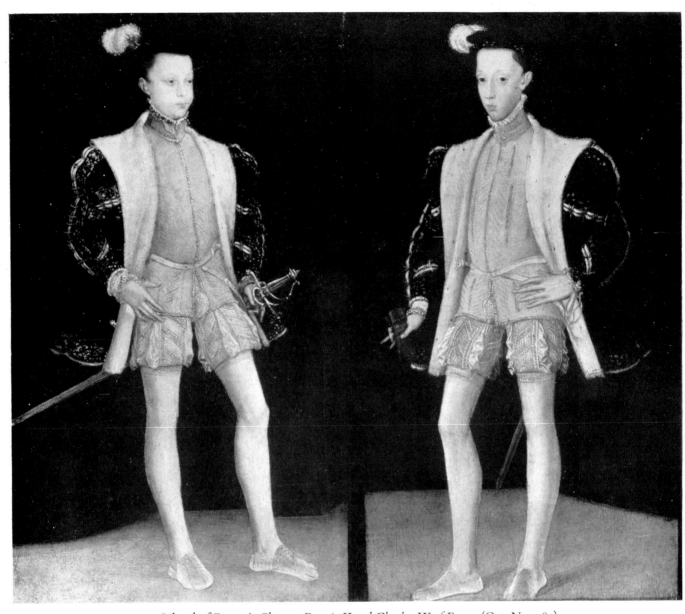

39. School of François Clouet: *Francis II and Charles IX of France* (Cat. No. 180)

40. School of Hans Holbein the Younger: *King Edward VI* (Cat. No. 192)

LORD CROMWELL   HOLBEIN

41. Hans Holbein the Younger: *Sir George Nevill, 5th Lord Abergavenny* (Drawing No. 18)

42. Jan Cornelisz Vermeyen: *Portrait of a Man* (Cat. No. 133)

43. Pieter Brueghel the Younger: 'The Bird Trap' (Cat. No. 143)

44. Jan Brueghel: *Winter Scene in a Village* (Cat. No. 144)

45. Sir Peter Paul Rubens: *Landscape with a Shepherd* (Cat. No. 155)

46. Sir Peter Paul Rubens: *Christ, St John and Two Angels* (Cat. No. 154)

47. Sir Peter Paul Rubens after Federigo Barocci: *The Martyrdom of St Vitalis* (Drawing No. 31)

48. After Sir Peter Paul Rubens: *The Assumption of the Virgin* (Cat. No. 156)

49. Frans Francken the Younger: *Interior of a Picture Gallery* (Cat. No. 148)

50. Artus Wolffordt: *A Seraglio, or the Bath* (Cat. No. 176)

51. Anglo-Dutch School, XVII Century: *King Charles I and Queen Henrietta Maria with William, 3rd Earl of Pembroke,*
Lord Steward, and his brother Philip, 1st Earl of Montgomery, Lord Chamberlain, inside Whitehall Palace or Durham House
(Cat. No. 141)

52. Frans Francken the Younger: *Interior of a Picture Gallery* (Detail of Cat. No. 148)

54. Sir Anthony van Dyck: *Queen Henrietta Maria* (Cat. No. 165)

53. Sir Anthony van Dyck: *King Charles I* (Cat. No. 164)

55. Sir Anthony van Dyck: *Charles, Prince of Wales, James, Duke of York, and Princess Mary, the three eldest children of King Charles I and Queen Henrietta Maria* (Cat. No. 166)

56. Sir Anthony van Dyck: *Mary Villiers, Duchess of Richmond, and Mrs Gibson, the Dwarf* (Cat. No. 163)

57. Sir Anthony van Dyck: *Elizabeth, Countess of Peterborough* (Cat. No. 170)

58. Sir Anthony van Dyck: *The Earl and Countess of Bedford* (Cat. No. 167)

59. Sir Anthony van Dyck: *The Countess of Morton and Mrs Killigrew* (Cat. No. 168)

60. Sir Anthony van Dyck: *The Duc d'Epernon* (Cat. No. 171)

61. Alexander Keirincx: *Cephalus and Procris* (Cat. No. 151)

62. Roelandt Savery: *St John preaching* (Cat. No. 125)

63. David Teniers the Younger: *The Pipe Smoker* (Cat. No. 174)

64. Egbert van Heemskerk the Elder: *Interior of a Farm House* (Cat. No. 110)

66. Gerrit van Honthorst: *Princess Sophia of Bohemia* (Cat. No. 113)

65. Gerrit van Honthorst: *Prince Rupert* (Cat. No. 112)

67. Abraham Bloemaert: *Shepherd and Shepherdess* (Cat. No. 103)

68. School of Frans Hals: *A Man amusing Children with a Rummel Pot* (Cat. No. 107)

69. Hendrick van Steenwijck: *The Liberation of St Peter* (Cat. No. 128)

70. Richard Brakenburgh: *Interior of a School* (Cat. No. 105)

71. Cornelis van Poelenburgh: *Landscape with Figures* (Cat. No. 122)

72. Gerard Ter Borch: *Battle Scene* (Cat. No. 104)

73. Caspar Netscher: *Portrait of a Man* (Cat. No. 121)

74. Gerard Ter Borch: *A Young Man seated astride a Rock* (Drawing No. 35)

75. Gerard Soest: *Portrait of a Young Man* (Cat. No. 127)

76. Willem van de Velde the Younger: *Shipping in a Calm* (Cat. No. 130)

77. Willem van de Velde the Younger: *Shipping in a Calm* (Cat. No. 131)

78. Jan van der Heyden: *The Church of St Michael, Antwerp* (Cat. No. 111)

79. Jan Ten Compe: *Almshouses on the River Amstel, Amsterdam* (Cat. No. 106)

80. Luca Signorelli: *St John the Divine writing* (Drawing No. 32)

81. Lorenzo Lotto: *The Assumption of the Virgin* (Cat. No. 209)

82. Lorenzo Lotto: *St Anthony the Hermit* (Cat. No. 208)

83. Gianfrancesco Penni: *The Holy Family with the Lamb* (Cat. No. 215)

84. Cesare da Sesto: *Leda and the Swan* (Cat. No. 224)

85. Andrea del Sarto: *The Virgin and Child, St John, a young Woman and Child* (Cat. No. 221)

86. Andrea del Sarto or Bacchiacca: *Christ bearing the Cross* (Cat. No. 222)

87. Raphael: *Head of a Cardinal* (Drawing No. 26)

88. Giovanni Girolamo Savoldo: *A Piper* (Cat. No. 223)

89. By or after Correggio: *Head of a Putto* (Drawing No. 8)

90. After Giulio Romano: *Head of Justice* (Drawing No. 30)

91. Tintoretto: *Christ washing the Disciples' Feet* (Cat. No. 218)

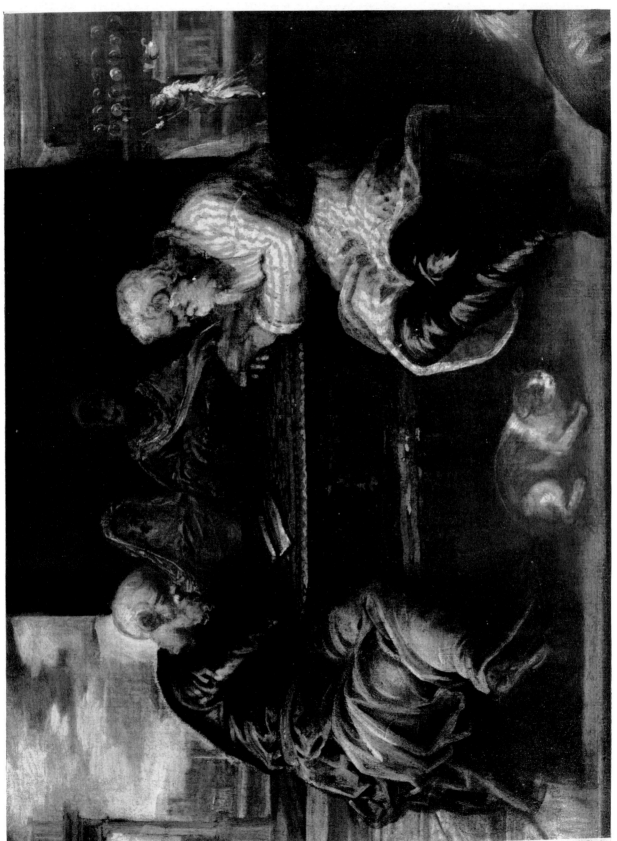

92. Tintoretto: *Christ washing the Disciples' Feet* (Detail of Cat. No. 218)

93. Jacopo Palma: *Soldiers disputing over Christ's Garments* (Cat. No. 213)

94. Tintoretto: *Christ washing the Disciples' Feet* (Detail of Cat. No. 218)

95. Attributed to Antonio Tempesta: *A Knight in Armour on a rearing Horse* (Drawing No. 34A)

96. Attributed to Antonio Tempesta: *Orpheus playing a 'Lira da Braccio', and a Maiden dancing* (Drawing No. 34B)

97. Michelangelo Cerquozzi: *Landscape with Figures* (Cat. No. 203)

98. Pietro Berettini da Cortona: *The Rape of the Sabines* (Cat. No. 204)

99. Salvator Rosa: *Landscape with Figures* (Cat. No. 219)

100. Pier Francesco Mola: *Bacchus and Ariadne* (Cat. No. 212)

101. Andrea Sacchi: *Job with his Wife and Friends* (Cat. No. 220)

102. G. B. Salvi (Sassoferrato) and Mario de' Fiori: *The Madonna* (Cat. No. 220A)

103. Italian (?), XVII Century: *Apollo and Marsyas* (Drawing No. 1)

104. Carlo Dolci: *An Apostle* (Drawing No. 12)

105. Carlo Dolci: *Bust of St John the Divine* (Drawing No. 13)

106. Benedetto Luti: *Head and shoulders of a young Woman* (Drawing No. 19)

107. Rosalba Carriera: *A Cupid lying on Clouds* (Drawing No. 6)

108. Francesco Solimena: *The Nativity* (Drawing No. 33)

109. Giuseppe Maria Crespi: *A Group of Market People* (Cat. No. 205)

110. Antonio Viviano: *Harbour Scene* (Cat. No. 227)

III. Gian Paolo Panini: *Ruins with Figures* (Cat. No. 214)

112. Jusepe Ribera: *Democritus* (Cat. No. 238)

113. Nicolas Poussin: *Two Putti* (Cat. No. 187)

114. Claude Lorraine: *Landscape with a Tree* (Cat. No. 185)

115. Jacques Courtois: *Battle Scene* (Cat. No. 181)

116. Claude-Joseph Vernet: *Harbour Scene* (Cat. No. 189)

117. Antoine Coypel: *A young Zephyr playing a Pipe* (Drawing No 10)

118. Antoine Coypel: *Head of a Woman in a Turban* (Drawing No. 11)

119. Martin Maingaud: *Frederick, Prince of Wales, Princess Anne (the Princess Royal), Princess Amelia Sophia Eleanor, and Princess Caroline Elizabeth* (Cat. No. 193)

120. Antoine Watteau: *A Country Boy, wearing a three-cornered Hat*
(Drawing No. 36)

121. Philippe Mercier: *A Musical Family* (Cat. No. 186)

122. Michael Dahl: *John, 2nd Duke of Montagu*, K.G. (Cat. No. 17)

123. School of Lely: *Portrait of a Man* (Cat. No. 46)

124-125. Samuel Scott: *Lincoln's Inn Fields* (Cat. No. 77) and *Covent Garden* (Cat. No. 78)

126. Samuel Scott: *Engagement between the Sloop H.M.S. 'Blast' and two Spanish Privateers* (Cat. No. 79)

127. Richard Wilson: *The Tomb of the Horatii and Curatii* (Cat. No. 89)

128. Richard Wilson: *Ariccia: A Fallen Tree* (Cat. No. 91)

129. William Hoare: *Henry, 9th Earl of Pembroke*
(Drawing No. 15)

130. William Hoare: *Mary Fitzwilliam, Countess of Pembroke*
(Drawing No. 16)

131. William Hoare: *Henry, Lord Herbert, their son*
(Drawing No. 17)

132. Johann Zoffany: *North Ludlow Bernard* (Cat. No. 93)

133. Sir Joshua Reynolds: *Augustus Hervey, 3rd Earl of Bristol* (Cat. No. 67)

134. Sir Joshua Reynolds: *Charles, 3rd Duke of Marlborough* (Cat. No. 68)

136. Sir Joshua Reynolds: *Lord Charles Spencer* (Cat. No. 70)

135. Sir Joshua Reynolds: *George, 4th Duke of Marlborough* (Cat. No. 69)

138. Sir Thomas Lawrence: *Count Simon Woronzow* (Cat. No. 40)

137. Frank Howard: *Prince Michael Woronzow* (Cat. No. 30)

139–140. Baron Reis d'Eisenberg: *Haute École: The Spanish Riding School* (Cat. No. 2)

141. Baron Reis d'Eisenberg: *Haute École: The Spanish Riding School* (Cat. No. 2)

142. Edward Pierce: *Hunting Scene* (in the Hunting Room)

143. Edward Pierce: *Hunting Scene* (in the Hunting Room)

144. Edward Pierce: *Hunting Scene* (in the Hunting Room)

145. Edward Pierce: *Hunting Scene* (in the Hunting Room)

146. Edward Pierce: *Hunting Scene* (in the Hunting Room)

147. Edward Pierce: *Hunting Scene* (in the Hunting Room)

148. Andien de Clermont: '*Singerie*' (Ceiling in the Colonnade Room)

INDEX OF PORTRAITS

INDEX OF ARTISTS

INDEX OF PORTRAITS

The numbers are those of the Catalogue entries, not those of the pages.

Rembrandt's mother, 124
Richmond and Lennox, Duchess of, 163
Richmond and Lennox, James Duke of, 172
Rockingham, Catherine Countess of, 45
Rupert, Prince, 112

Sawyer, Margaret, see Margaret, Countess of Pembroke
Sidney, Philip, 139
Slingsby, Barbara, see Barbara, Countess of Pembroke
Sophia, Princess of Bohemia, 113
Spencer, Elizabeth, see Elizabeth, Countess of Pembroke
Spencer, Lord Charles, 70
Spencer, Georgina Countess, 200
Spiller, Jane, 42

Talbot, Gertrude, see Gertrude, Countess of Pembroke
Tremamondo, Domenico Angelo Malevolti, 47, 51

Villiers, Anne, see Morton
Villiers, Catherine, see Catherine, Countess of Pembroke
Villiers, Lady Mary, 158
Villiers, Mary, Duchess of Richmond and Lennox, 163

Wilson, Lelia, 184
Woodroffe, Benjamin, 29
Woronzow, Catherine, see Catherine, Countess of Pembroke
Woronzow, Michael, 30, 195
Woronzow, Simon, 40
Wrettle, Mrs. 25

INDEX OF ARTISTS

The numbers are those of the Catalogue entries, not those of the pages.